**Abigail Ahern** is an interior design powerhouse, retailer, influential tastemaker and 'style spotter extraordinaire' (*The Times*). Her trendsetting designs are synonymous with glamour, eclecticism and wit. In 2015, she launched the Abigail Ahern own-label collection, available worldwide, and her Abigail Ahern London store. She is the author of the bestselling *Everything*, a guest judge on *Interior Design Masters* with Alan Carr (BBC/Netflix) and regularly appears on radio and TV offering her interiors expertise.

# ABIGAIL AHERN
# MASTERCLASS

# ABIGAIL AHERN
# MASTERCLASS

PAVILION

# CONTENTS

# INTRODUCTION

The furniture is in, the cushions are plumped, the shelves are up – but something is missing. What is it? Your house may be rocking all those design-magazine clichés like Moroccan rugs and blush-painted walls, never mind the ubiquitous console, plus oversized mirror, plus lamp combo in the hallway, yet something still feels wrong. It doesn't make you feel particularly happy, so what on earth is missing? Magic – that's what.

In this book I'll be taking interiors to a whole different level by doing away with the cookie-cutter approach to design and instead navigating a new language that encourages everyone to become risk-takers, storytellers, rule-breakers and magicians.

Delving deeper than ever before into elements that can make such a dramatic difference to our homes, I'll be looking at how to combine polarizing qualities, and drilling down into all those components that are often neglected in order to demystify them. From key furniture arrangements and fail-safe magical formulas for surfaces, to cracking the code on mixing and matching lighting; from 'fake it till you make it' flooring to stylish statements with tiles, as well as remedies for renters, there are infinite ways to spice things up. Creating pleasing, memorable spaces that are original, showstopping and offer a new kind of visual lexicon takes quite a bit of skill, but don't worry – I'll be whipping out all my wisdom and know-how, and imparting the tips, tricks and insider knowledge that I've shared in the international masterclasses I've run over many years.

*One of my all-time magical formulas – and it's as fail-safe as they come – is restricting the number of colours in a room. The colours used in this space add up to no more than four different hues. I might go up and down with the saturation level of a hue, but I keep the overall number really restricted.*

I'll be breaking down the details of a room, decoding and distilling everything piece by piece, providing you with all the tools necessary to make your space as fabulous and thoughtfully pulled together as possible. Coming from a place of wanting to help, I will encourage you while gently pushing you to decorate differently. My aim is to give you the confidence to transform your space into something swoon-worthy. To this day I adore receiving emails, messages and pictures of people's homes, seeing how they've transformed them into something truly magical.

You can dip in and out of this book, knowing it will be just as relevant in the years to come as it is today. I want you to feel almost as if I'm in the room with you, willing you to take a risk. Without wanting to sound like a teacher (and this is definitely not a replacement for college), I want this book to be where learning and entertaining intersect. There is certainly skill involved when it comes to mixing unexpected elements together to achieve a vibe that is fanciful yet friendly, but it's so achievable when you know how. At the end of all this, I would love nothing more than for you to feel totally comfortable putting coral cushions on a toffee-coloured sofa, next to a side table with a sequinned vase. Or perhaps choosing to place a *fin de siècle* Parisian-style lamp on a modern table, alongside a leopard-print pouffe with a beautiful dhurrie skimming the floor beneath it.

*Right: In my book you can never have enough table lamps – they create beautiful pockets of glow, so overdose on them.*

*Far right: When you echo the palette and use tonal shades throughout, a space will always work.*

Creating idiosyncratic spaces does, of course, take experience. Remember that my eye, which is super-exacting and precise, has been trained over many years. I've overseen zillions of store revamps, not to mention trade shows all over the world, plus the design of countless residential and commercial spaces, and all this has given me an innate understanding of how a space should feel. In a nutshell: relaxed, lived-in, loved, grand and yet super-effortless. Interiors, for me, are an endless love affair and I'm incredibly excited to be able to share my knowledge of a host of game-changing touches with this book. Creating a beautiful room packed with things, which looks busy without being forced, is actually not as hard as it seems. The bottom line is that I've gone out of my way to give you the best learning materials possible so that you'll be able to shake things up. You'll be blending diverse influences in next to no time, and taking practical steps that will literally turn your interiors around.

I have also highlighted trusted voices from within the industry (creatives, tastemakers and designers), from Jason Atherton and his beautiful London home to Jeremiah Brent and Nate Berkus's phenomenal New York brownstone – one of the most pinned interiors out there. Whether you want warm and homely or attention-grabbing and glam, rustic or clean-lined and elegant, get your loungewear ready and welcome in your trusted filter, guide and BFF on all things decorating.

It's good to be home.

*Left: There's such a thoughtful quietness to this vignette. Playing upon the aesthetic known as Japandi (a calming fusion of Scandinavian and Japanese style), which is greatly influenced by the ancient Japanese philosophy of wabi-sabi, a way of life that embraces slowing down and surrounding yourself with pieces imbued with comfort and cosiness, like these ceramics and textiles.*

*Opposite: This free-spirited approach to decorating embraces a modern bohemia, layering different styles in a beautifully curated fashion.*

Introduction

# PERFECT PERCHES

From gallery-worthy chaises to chairs, pouffes and the sofa's little sister, the occasional bench, seating can dramatically change the way you interact with your space. No matter how large or small your home, having a place to chill, read or recline that doesn't involve retreating under the duvet is all good in my book.

Whether you fancy something opulent and upholstered, sleek, rugged, mid-century or classic, for as much as two-thirds of the day our bottoms are sat firmly on a seat, which makes selecting these perches one of the most important decorating decisions you are ever going to make. No pressure then. And I haven't even started on alternative seating options like stools, pillows and cushions – budget-friendly alternatives and go-to solutions when dinner guests unexpectedly bring their friends and you need way more seating than originally planned.

Growing up in our house, my parents always had sofas and chairs that beckoned you to sprawl: deep, squidgy armchairs and couches that made me feel protected and supported. Now, 30-plus years on, I've embraced seating that does the very same thing; it feels relaxed and lived-in. In my house you'll find lots of intimate conversational areas that put me and my guests instantly at ease. There is no one particular style – I have a mixed bag including streamlined bouclé seating, cashmere-velvet traditional sofas and even loveseats upholstered with rugs. There are leather chairs I've found at flea markets, vintage 1970s plastic chairs I've picked up off the street, and even a rocking chair crafted from concrete that came from an uber-cool gallery some years ago. It was the first chair I ever bought and I love it just as much now as I did then. I also have bits of wood I use as benches and stools, and oversized pouffes that double as coffee tables and impromptu seating. As I take you through selecting the perfect perch, you'll see it's all about having different styles from a range of eras and budgets.

I will also be looking at how to arrange your perches. Get it right, and it will make relaxing feel more restorative, dinner parties more fun, working from home easier, hallways far cooler, bedrooms more stylish – and there is still a whole bunch of rooms to go! Not only will you feel uplifted, but along the way you'll create a home that brings you a deep sense of wellbeing, and a place you never want to leave. All of this from sorting your seating. Clever, hey?

*Squishy upholstered dining chairs united in colour dramatically up the cosiness of this kitchen.*

Perfect perches

# TAKE A SEAT

First things first: when considering seating options, break down your spaces into zones and then work out all the possibilities you might need to create the most beautiful, welcoming space imaginable. Go beyond just being practical. This doesn't mean you have to start from scratch, but if, for example, your room is feeling a little off, more often than not it's the perches that will be throwing things out. I've added little stools to landings, the odd occasional chair to a bedroom and a super-sweet bench next to a bath, and this has transformed those spaces. Seating will help dictate the mood, so if you don't have enough, it can feel sterile; on the other hand, too many large pieces can make a room feel unbalanced, cramped and claustrophobic. A common mistake I see time and time again is a lack of variety or, in many cases, not enough seating options.

In a nutshell, we have to be strategic and think constantly about variety. Accent chairs aren't just reserved for living rooms, they are also fabulous in kitchens, bathrooms, hallways and bedrooms because they give you the excuse to play with texture, colour and pattern. They will also give you somewhere to put a bag, clothes, or yourself, and are a great way to inject more style, and of course function, into areas you might previously have ignored.

When it comes to living rooms, having choice is key, so always consider stools, benches, pouffes, ottomans and low-backed chairs to create a space that feels layered. In dining rooms always mix up chair styles; consider, for example, adding long upholstered benches to dining tables (these also work well in hallways and landings).

Some pieces beckon us to sprawl while others offer us support. Both are equally important. Your goal is to have as many seating options as you possibly can as it will encourage you to linger longer and will create instant pockets of cosiness.

*Left: Comfortable chairs that invite guests to linger are just as important as a killer playlists and flowing vino. This earthy green upholstery connects with the outdoors beautifully.*

*Opposite: Chairs are the unsung heroes of any room. Aesthetics aside – and they are, of course, super-important – the perfect seat (whether at the dining table or by the fire) has to embrace you with a curvy frame, a soft touch and a welcoming delicacy.*

# CREATE A
# SIGNATURE
# FEELING

*Giving an area a unique point of view by playing
with colour and scale offers a change in perspective,
creating the ultimate conversational piece.*

It's not so much about creating a signature style, but a signature feeling. When it comes to designing it's not just about how a room looks. It's all about developing a process and creating a room's mood. Aside from the visuals, how does it feel to the touch, or smell? Does the materiality excite, do the textures tantalize, does the furniture beckon you to linger longer? Do the colours feel restorative and comforting or exciting and intriguing? There is so much to consider.

*Design is very much an expression of your style – surrounding yourself with pieces, colour palettes and materials that you love. This is how you create a signature feeling.*

*The most succinct way to express your personality at home is to layer ingredients – materials, colour palettes and accessories – to achieve a bespoke look that reads as cohesive and considered.*

# LET'S START WITH SOFAS

Sofas are one of the hardest-working, expensive and emotionally loaded pieces you will ever buy. They have a huge impact when it comes to creating a mood as they occupy a lot of space and visual weight, so getting them right is key. They are the primary hang-out place, so need to be both stylish and functional. I can remember when we had to choose ours, 20-odd years ago (yes, it has lasted that long) – it felt like a minefield.

There are so many types to choose from, from sectionals and loveseats to sofa beds and chaises. When it comes to styles, the options are equally vast: English roll arm (that's us), Chesterfields, camelbacks, tuxedos, chaises, and not forgetting mid-century modern. Mid-centuries are all about clean lines and tapered legs with a tufted back; English roll arms have deep seats, tucked arms, soft curves and are super-versatile; Chesterfields have tufted accents and nail-head detailing; tuxedos are streamlined and composed; camelbacks have a gorgeous arched back that reaches a higher point on either side; while chaises are a cross between a loveseat and an accent chair.

Now let's talk upholstery and lifestyle: velvet, velvet-cashmere (us again) wool, linen, leather, natural fibres, synthetics – I could go on and on. Kids, pets, sun exposure and amount of use are all key factors in making your selection as, of course, is the budget. From experience, if you can, don't go for the cheap option: a quality sofa lasts a lifetime – ours is 23 years old and has never been re-upholstered. Vintage is also always worth keeping an eye out for. Buying a sofa is an investment, and not only that, it sets the foundation and is the key unifying piece that ties all the other elements of the space together.

*When you tie in the colour of a large piece of furniture like a sofa to the colour palette of the rest of the room, you immediately take the space to a new level of sophistication.*

# THE MAGIC FORMULA

The magic formula when choosing a sofa is to make sure it doesn't overwhelm the space, and if you have more than one sofa in a room, think about outlines. If one sofa is curvaceous, the other should be long and low; if one has legs, the other should skim the floor. Never match shapes if possible.

The thing I consider most important when selecting a sofa is comfort. My days are long, so by the evening I need something squidgy and supremely comfortable to fall into. From movie nights with a glass of wine, to kicked-back after-dinner conversations, to slouching around in PJs on a Sunday afternoon with a book, I want a sofa that invites me to sprawl but also makes me feel supported. I generally opt for deep-seaters, so English roll arms are my go-to types, but that does mean my other smaller sofa and chair types need to vary – companionable in, say, materiality or even colour, but different in style. So, I might opt for chairs and stools that are a little more upright, and that way the sofas and chairs in my repertoire feel spontaneous and well considered, not matchy-matchy or too perfectly done!

Sofas are not just for living rooms either. I've got sofas and chairs in bedrooms, and many people these days are re-imagining kitchens and plopping couches and chairs into spaces where they cook and eat. With banquettes, settles and loveseats, kitchens have become much less of a place purely to prepare and cook food, and more of a space to gather and relax.

*Left: Swooping silhouettes and luxurious materials like the richly inky weaves on these sofas always read as sophisticated, particularly when you restrict the palette as much as this.*

*Overleaf: Patterns or not? On large pieces like sofas, for longevity and sustainability it's best to opt for plain weaves in durable fabrics that best fit your lifestyle. Throw in some pillowy, slouchy cushions and you've nailed it.*

My days are long, so by the evening I need something squidgy and supremely comfortable to fall into.

# POWER COUPLES

It's hard to even know where to begin with chairs. From armchairs to occasional chairs to dining chairs, these versatile pieces are where we collapse after a long day, sit down for breakfast, lunch and supper, and relax into with a book. I think of them as an integral accessory. Forget the practical for a minute, and instead concentrate on the form, the size and the vibe, all of which will contribute to dictating the mood of a space. Look on them as the perfect design tool because they can add so much sass to any space. Mix them up as much as you can and let loose with styles and materials: from 1950s Italian leather to concrete Willy Guhl Loop chairs, or from an animal print to a reclining number in velvet. With literally thousands to choose from, be they classic or contemporary, know that chairs are to interiors what shoes are to fashion. They make or break a look!

Let's start with armchairs. The three-piece suite is long gone; these days no one matches chairs to sofas, and secondary seating in a different style and fabric is the name of the game. Ask any interior designer to name their number-one backbone piece in a room and the answer will always be the armchair. They are the building blocks of the decorating world and there is nothing quite like unwinding into one.

As with sofas, the options are endless: curvy, boxy, arms, no arms. Wingbacks, high backs, recliners, not to mention modern silhouettes, innovative materials, contemporary upholstery: there are so many possibilities. Aside from considering how you will be using your chairs – which will, of course, determine the shape (do you like sitting with feet up, curled under, legs out?) – remember always to create contrast between your chair options and your sofa options. For example, if you have a velvet sofa, try not to go for velvet chairs. Go for linen, wool or any other contrasting fabric, and layer up or down with cushions and throws according to the seasons.

Buddying up armchairs with sofas is no easy task as there's a lot to think about. There is no fancy algorithm or hard-and-fast rule for finding the perfect match, but don't panic – the guidelines that follow will help.

Perfect perches

*Above left: Doubling up on key pieces like armchairs makes a sculptural statement. These low-slung armchairs are big on style and comfort.*

*Above: A structured dining chair hanging out next to a pedestal table is my idea of heaven. You want to mix things up constantly, and this curvy, chunky table offset by the more delicate leggy chairs is the perfect combo in my book.*

# CHOOSING
# CHAIRS

A truly welcoming occasional chair should tempt you to linger
longer. Partner it with a side table and you've suddenly created
the sweetest little vignette. I also adore the interplay here
between the solid oak table and both chairs.

You can never go wrong with a voluptuous,
sculptural, low-slung chair – it always adds
so much dimension to a room.

My biggest piece of advice when choosing chairs, and especially when pairing sofas with chairs, is to create some contrast, no matter how small. Whether that's through colour, shape, style, form or materiality, contrast is the name of the game. See my tips on the next page.

*The same style of chair around a table in a luxe fabric always looks beautiful. Adding a different fabric to the chair at the end keeps things fresh, making this space an inviting spot to settle into.*

## Avoid matching chairs to sofas

The trouble with matching styles, fabrics and materiality is that, more often than not, the room will feel flat and one-dimensional. Mixing styles is key: remember, it doesn't have to be dramatic, as subtle contrasts in shape, fabric and texture will look just as beautiful.

## Consider scale

While I am all for playing around with scale and varying it when it comes to combining sofas and chairs, I do feel they should complement one another in size and proportion – it will throw the room off if your sofa is super-huge and your chairs are bijou. Having said that, a well-chosen chair of substantial size will add a stylish update to any other space, such as a kitchen, bedroom or bathroom, especially if that room lacks many other seating options.

## Consider colour and texture

When it comes to selecting chair colours, once again there are so many choices. Weave together opposite shades to your sofa; go brighter, darker or lighter for a bigger impact. Often, opting for chairs with a punchier vibe breathes new life into interiors and adds visual interest. I love to pick out colour themes and restrict the palette. Always consider other textiles in the room, from rugs to cushions and curtains, when considering the upholstery. Work out if you want to contrast or complement, and go as textural as you dare, with rich velvets, bouclé, cord and slubby wools.

## Let's talk legs and form

If your sofa is boxy with short legs, as many of them are, then consider going for chairs with a longer leg profile or no legs at all because this will help the visual balance. You can also contrast leg styles between a number of chairs as this little detail creates a lovely, intriguing accent.

## Pairs don't need to be twins

Try coupling a matching pair of armchairs for a cohesive effect, or mixing them up and not worrying about them having to match – they absolutely don't have to. None of mine match and they co-exist happily because I've reduced the number of colours in the room, making mixing different styles a breeze.

*In design you want to create – as odd as this may sound – as much friction between materiality, texture and colour as possible. So a super-glam gold chair next to a darker metal desk nails it!*

# UNPREDICTABILITY PLAYS A KEY ROLE

When it comes to combining dining chairs, occasional chairs and benches, think unexpected juxtapositions and friction. Friction plays an important role in interior design, one that many people don't even notice. You create friction by mixing up styles, finishes and materials; it keeps things interesting, spicing up an interior. Whether it's wooden or fabric chairs, choosing between metal or plastic, or even upholstered benches, contrasts are key in elevating a room.

Rather than picking a single style that reads as very one-note, vary the design of seats around a room or table. Embrace the fear of commitment and becoming locked into a single style by switching and mixing everything up. I'm talking different heights, different widths, arms vs armless, upholstered seats vs hard seats – and remember, opposites always attract.

There are three main ways to go with dining chairs: all matching; matching but just down the side of a table with different chairs at the head; or eclectic, where no two chairs are the same. Personally, I would encourage you to go for contrast, so plump either for matching at the sides with different options at the head, or full-on eclectic.

You can mismatch every chair, but I mismatch in pairs so that it feels less jumbly and more considered. It gives me the contrast I crave to keep things interesting but it doesn't feel messy. Do that and everything will look like it belongs around the table. You can pair wooden with upholstered; clean lines with elegant; or mid-century with industrial. You can combine overly artistic silhouettes with super-streamlined ones, or shiny Lucite (a type of acrylic) with fabric. Interesting textures take things up a notch, too, like cane, leather, silk, wool, nubby bouclé, grainy and varied woods, or quiet flaxes – complement and contrast away. Just remember to keep some unity within the colour palette for cohesion.

You could also stick to one key shape but vary the colours and textures; restaurants do this a lot, and it always feels super-cool.

I also love a chair and bench mash-up around a table as this screams risk-taker! Free-floating benches along one side of a dining table add instant variation. The long silhouette is also great for seating lots of people, and you never have to worry about co-ordinating your bench with existing chairs, as it can work as a statement piece in its own right. Plus, benches can go anywhere if you get bored of them around the table: at the foot of a bed, in the hallway, against a wall with art above – they are incredibly versatile.

*Cosy, low-slung chairs happily tick all the boxes, combining comfort with craftsmanship.*

*Pleasingly curvaceous with its generous proportions, this rattan armchair would add a sculptural presence to any space.*

# THE EXTRA SEATERS

Pouffes, oversized cushions, ottomans and stools all make fabulous seating but they are often underappreciated. In my book they're one of the most important decorating staples out there. Portable, small, stylish and at a wide range of different price points, they can flank sofas, sit alongside chairs, do double duty as coffee tables – these multifaceted pieces enhance interiors in so many ways. Whether they're made of fabric, leather or wood, they provide instant versatility, and effortless additional seating.

In terms of style, these seaters can be anything from upholstered X-benches to Moroccan pouffes and stools. I love them for this reason alone – you can see straight over them, so they never block the view, and they almost always seem to disappear. Keeping sight lines uninterrupted is a big plus. Another perk is that their size allows you to stow them under tables. A fail-safe decorating trick is to place them under consoles, adding a pleasingly layered effect, which is beautiful in hallways and dining rooms.

Pair them up as part of a focal point, split them up, dot them around bedrooms, on landings, everywhere and anywhere. They add so much to a space without overwhelming it, providing not just a place to plop down, but a wonderful structural element as well.

*Left: I love doubling up on stools, and it always works when you play with the heights. Being narrow and low, they can be tucked under consoles when not in use, which is something I do often.*

*Opposite: Stools are so versatile, changing form and function as they go, from a place to perch impromptu guests to a table flanking a sofa, to housing the TV at the end of the bed. They can be placed anywhere – bathrooms, landings, hallways – and be styled with or without accessories.*

# SEATING SET-UPS THAT WON'T FAIL

During all my years in the design biz, one of the biggest challenges I faced was helping people to think differently about furniture layouts. More often than not, these are an afterthought, a no-brainer: sofas shoved against walls facing the TV or fireplace with a coffee table in the middle was pretty much the norm. There might be some built-in storage and a few chairs off to the side, but it can be so much more than that.

The most successful furniture layouts cater to the way we live, with areas for entertaining and face-to-face yabbering, mixed with quiet spots for contemplation. I know this might sound super-weird, but I want to encourage you to think almost like a poet or a writer when it comes to layout. Think about drawing people into your space with interesting grouping arrangements, which engage, tantalize, excite and intrigue. I'm talking about the sensation you get when you go to see a play or read a great book. I happen to think that knowing that you can, albeit subconsciously, lift someone's spirits by getting the layout of a room on point is so exciting.

Start by asking as many questions as possible. Designers do this all the time and it's a great way to understand what you want from your layout and why.

*It may seem counterintuitive to position chairs away from the wall, but doing so even slightly will make your room flow better, giving it more space to breathe. Plus it encourages conversation. Win-win!*

Perfect perches

## Seating checklist

☐ What is the vision you have for your layout? As obvious as this sounds, if you put together a mood board or source images online beforehand, it will guide you and help you to focus.

☐ There are zillions of home-layout tools you can use, such as magicplan, RoomScan Pro, Planner 5D and Room Creator Interior Design (to name just a few) that can help with layout and configuration. Designing rooms isn't easy, and at times it's hard to visualize the end result, but with online room planners you can create the perfect layout!

☐ Drill down into your habits. Do you read a lot (in which case, creating cosy reading nooks is key)? Do you entertain much, use the room for work, to relax over coffee? Thinking about your lifestyle is vital in getting the layout right as it contributes to creating a space that is truly yours.

☐ Having said that, don't get too stuck if things are not working in the way you want. If this is the case, move a chair or re-orientate the sofa, and this will give your pad a whole new lease of life.

*When it comes to choosing seating there are so many things to consider. Not only are upholstered pieces the focal point in a room, but also the main cosy spot to lounge, socialize and even work. Choosing neutral colours will have a unifying effect on the space, especially if it's already neutral.*

# The 10 commandments of furniture placement

1.  Go off the wall: put your furniture in the middle of the room.

2.  Include great focal points.

3.  Group seating to make conversation easy.

4.  Make traffic flow interesting by banning straight lines.

5.  Avoid complete symmetry in an arrangement. Always mix it up a bit.

6.  Use diagonals in a small space.

7.  Always pair a chair with a spot for a mug or lamp.

8.  Harness the magic of mirrors.

9.  Use rugs to anchor your space.

10. Create zones for different activities with clever lighting.

*Pulling furniture away from the walls, even just a little, will immediately make a space feel more inviting and cosy.*

Perfect perches

# The 10 commandments in detail

1. Before going any further, I'm going to get super-bossy and implore you not to push your furniture against the walls, no matter how small the space. If you do, you will get this weird dead space in the middle, and it will just feel wrong. I know this sounds counterintuitive, but your room will feel bigger if you let it breathe, and moving the sofa off even a tad will create a better sense of balance. No longer will you be highlighting a room's cramped dimensions. And if you happen to have a larger space, move the furniture into the middle of the room as quickly as you can!

2. To create a personality-packed layout, look at the bones of your room and decide what to highlight by selecting a main focal point. Focal points draw the eye instantly and can appear naturally, such as a fireplace mantel or a window. Or you can create your own by adding something the eye is immediately drawn to. You can go big with a mirror, large pendant or supersized plant; or you can go small with a vibrant cushion or a vase in an intoxicating hue.

Orientate the largest piece of furniture you have, which will be the sofa, towards this prominent feature and then position smaller seating options, such as stools and chairs, either opposite or adjacent. Finish off by adding in accent items like coffee tables, occasional tables and lamps.

Once you have your main focus, create two more secondary focal points. Do this and the eye won't know where to look when you first walk into the room, which is a good thing. With one focal point, once the eye has landed there is nowhere else to go; add in a few more and you'll be moving the eye around the room like a pro.

3. Conversational areas are fundamental in our super-busy, plugged-in world, so chairs and sofas need to be positioned near one another. In narrower rooms, choose leaner chairs without arms, and add pieces such as ottomans and stools to create additional perches. In larger rooms, establish multiple conversational areas by designating zones. Think about a variety of shapes and sizes to bring balance to the space.

4. Traffic flow is key, so make sure there's a clear path between pieces – no one wants bruised shins. Odd as this may sound, arrange furniture so you can't walk from one side of the room to the other in a straight line. The aim is to make people weave a little, so place things deliberately in the way. All the coolest retailers do this: it's called activating your peripheral vision. Paths should never be entirely straight, and, as I said in Commandment 1, furniture should not be banked against walls. Subconsciously this activates your senses and stimulates the brain.

**5.** Symmetrical layouts bring cohesion and balance to a room and create a sense of order, so typically seating pieces would face one another, with chairs paired opposite a sofa perhaps. Side tables can be matched, as can lamps, although OD-ing on symmetry makes rooms super-dull and uptight. If you are going for this arrangement, always only match one element like chairs or side tables, never everything. I prefer asymmetry: it is much harder to pull off, but so much cooler. Balance is just as important though, so tie everything together with colour, pattern and scale.

**6.** If a room is boxy, go diagonal with your layout. Diagonal arrangements add more dimension and intrigue. Use the sofa and coffee table to establish the diagonal axis and then arrange additional seating along that axis.

**7.** Create a more relaxed, laid-back room by dotting chairs about more randomly. So, with a sofa running lengthways and a coffee table in front of it, mix in mismatching chairs in spaces opposite, at angles and on corners. Always make sure every chair gets a buddy, too – a little table or stool where you can pop a coffee – or it will feel too lonesome.

**8.** Mirrors add depth, expand horizons and look magical, especially if you go big. Place one on a wall opposite a window and the light will bounce around and create the illusion that the room is much bigger than it really is. Oh, and win-win, your mirror can also act as one of your key focal points.

**9.** Anchor the space with a rug. Area rugs will stop a room looking like a furniture showroom as they ground, define and add texture and pattern to any space.

**10.** Break each space into zones. With large spaces, create numerous zones for reading, TV watching, entertaining, etc. With smaller spaces, clever styling can create the illusion of more space, as can multifunctional furniture. Create break points through lighting in these smaller spaces, making every inch count.

Remember, every commandment can be broken. If something isn't working, be rebellious, experiment, be creative and flout the rules!

# GETTING CREATIVE WITH PRINT AND PATTERN

Mixing patterns and even introducing print to sofas, chairs, benches, ottomans and cushions can feel intimating, but with a little insider knowledge you'll soon be mixing and layering patterns like a pro – I promise. Pattern plays such an important role in drawing a room together, making it appear welcoming, intriguing and compelling. I happen to think it's probably one of the most under-utilized components out there.

If everything in a room were a solid colour it would feel flat and energy-draining, so adding pattern, even in the smallest of ways, adds instant personality to a room.

Patterns also act as focal points, and when you contrast multiple patterns, it takes rooms to a whole new level. I love mixing patterns that feel like opposites. For example, I might have an animal-print bench, and then on a chair I might place a cushion in a super-cool floral print.

When it comes to choosing patterns, first determine the look you're after, then mix away: just be aware that the biggest print in the room will dictate the overall mood. Animal prints feel glam and quite eclectic; florals feel a little more free-flowing and soothing as they feature lots of circles and curves; and stripes, especially horizontal ones, are quite grounding.

*Pattern-packed furniture adds instant interest to a room. If everything is a solid hue it can feel a little draining. When it comes to mixing patterns, unify with colour – if they don't match, just make sure they relate in a subtle way.*

Never worry about which pattern goes with which; I like creating fabulous combos with any of these options: florals, stripes, polka dots, herringbone, paisley, ikat, geometrics and plaid. Just make sure you vary the scale, mixing in small cushions with bigger pieces like rugs. Balance is important, not just in the colours but in the locations of the prints, so always distribute your patterns evenly throughout the room for cohesion. As a general rule, use three patterns in a room – it's a simple strategy and it always works. Another sure-fire way to combine patterns successfully is to dial down the number of colours.

Mix in solids, too, to break up any expanse of pattern. I find that patterns are at their most magical when they have plenty of room to breathe.

*Opposite: The trick to using multiple patterns in a space is to keep a few unifying principles in mind. Restricting the palette and repeating similar patterns creates instant harmony.*

*Right: Wood grain and rattan make beautiful organic patterns in themselves. If you're scared of mixing patterns in fabric, go subtle as here so your eye feels comfortable and not overwhelmed.*

Perfect perches

# PUNCHING UP
# THE PALETTE

Perfect perches

Exploring new colour ideas with your seating is a stylish way of giving your room a jolt of personality. Suddenly, chairs, benches and sofas become way more interesting. Colour creates such visual interest, and as previously discussed, the key is not to match them. Get the colour right and it can lift your spirits and totally reinvent your space.

Rather than playing it safe, push your colour choices and avoid getting caught up in what's hot and what's not. Take risks, make it personal and go for it. Ask yourself if you want lively and contrasting, or calm and spa-like – there are plenty of different options.

Start small, maybe opting for a bench or small chair, and consider going dramatic. I happen to think that dark hues make any piece feel uber-sophisticated, chic and timeless – you can't really go wrong. The reason I'm so drawn to swampy, inky hues is that they make pieces feel super-glam and seductive, and these deep colours add a sense of luxury and mystery to a space, transmitting a powerful message.

*The beautiful patterned upholstery on the sofa is elevated by the dark background behind. Having that plain wall makes you focus on the pattern, giving it extra sharpness.*

That said, neutrals never fail, and you don't have to be a colour-phobe to embrace them. Taupes, khakis and rain-cloud greys all work beautifully together. Neutrals are a potent player in manipulating how a space feels and, unlike brighter hues, they never feel loud, aggressive or abrasive, no matter what shade you use – they always read as softly spoken, tranquil and restful. Seating is quite an investment, so you will never go wrong opting for neutrals.

Brights are also fabulous: the odd chair, bench or even sofa will pack a powerful punch if you go for a bright, compelling hue. I tend to use saturated colours in isolation, such as in cushions, ottomans and pouffes, but there is no wrong or right answer. I think the thing to remember with your seating pieces is that not everything has to be colourful. I use a lot of colours that don't fight for attention, giving my pad room to breathe.

Repeating colours throughout your seating repertoire will give your space extra kudos; echo sofa colours on a pouffe or floor cushion, for instance. It's a simple way to create instant harmony and cohesion. Whatever you go for, try and push the boundaries as much as you can. If your default is cautious, start experimenting with colour on smaller accent pieces. A trick I use time and time again is to pick a colour family and then go up and down the saturation level. Let's say my sofa is swampy green, so into this scheme I might add lime, sage, forest green, blue-green, pear, sea foam and olive with some of my accessories, and also other upholstered pieces. If it was brown, then I might add in baked clay, buff, chestnut, burnt umber, desert sand and chocolate, with benches and, again, with accessories. Can you see where I am going with this? Working with a colour family is so simple. In a nutshell, I am doing everything I can to ground the experience, making sure all my seating has some sort of commonality in terms of the visual, the tactile and the sensual.

*A easy way to create harmony in a space is to gently blend the colour scheme, as seen here, with the pinky brown tones that unite the wall, the chair and the softly woven rug.*

# NATE BERKUS AND JEREMIAH BRENT
## A New York City showstopper

*The grasscloth-covered walls in the living area create a tranquil mood, making this the perfect space to hunker down.*

Perfect perches

Vintage pieces are placed throughout Nate and Jeremiah's home and they add real soul. This stunning antique mirror expands the space, adding both depth and intrigue.

The muted shades embody tranquillity, and the beautifully layered interiors make it feel as if pieces have been gathered and assembled over time.

In the heart of Manhattan sits an oasis of a house belonging to the designers Nate Berkus and Jeremiah Brent and their two young children, Poppy and Oscar. Credited as the world's most recognizable interior designers, their work constantly features in leading publications around the globe.

'Showstopping' doesn't even begin to describe their home. Double-height bookcases, grasscloth wallcoverings, tailored upholstery; it's a space that is grand and beautiful, but also a home that makes you feel instantly at ease. I love how Nate and Jeremiah have created an environment that so harmoniously blends each of their points of view. The couple both have their own design firms, employing different styles, so what's clever (genius, actually) is how they've blended their personal aesthetics (traditional, modern, organic, earthy) to create this richly layered home.

Their home is such a calm retreat, and a contrast to the hustle of New York City. The muted shades embody tranquillity, and the beautifully layered interiors make it feel as if pieces have been gathered and assembled over time. Everything feels cohesive, effortless and elegant. It's also a very artisanal home, with varied surfaces, interesting textiles, beautiful ceramics, woods, metals and so many other natural materials on constant replay throughout. It's such a handsome abode, too, with some lovely architectural details, such as mantels, the white oak double-height bookcase, steel-framed glazed doors and interesting light fixtures, all of which contrast with the sharp lines of the furniture and the beautiful upholstery.

A deep sense of calm pervades many of the rooms, apart from the children's bedrooms, which are more lively and vibrant. One of

*Opposite: A showstopping double-height bookcase adds immense warmth to the family's living room and showcases their collection of books, framed photographs and pottery beautifully.*

*Below: Chalk walls, sculptural trees, and the use of wood, stone and ceramic create a beautiful timeworn feel.*

Perfect perches

Perfect perches

the most colourful spaces belongs to their daughter Poppy. Her bedroom rocks an eye-catching floral wallpaper, deeply plush pink carpet and a beautiful pink velvet bedframe.

It's the layered approach that is so clever – that, and the fact that there are no trendy, impersonal items on display; you feel that every piece has a meaning and tells a story. I think that is Nate and Jeremiah's forté: creating inspiring, tantalizing interiors filled with such items as hand-loomed textiles and handcrafted tables – pieces that have a patina and carry a narrative.

Nothing feels too precious and everything feels incredibly individual. When you look around, your eye doesn't quite know where to land first – everything looks intriguing, yet is coupled with a sense of comfort. When you fill a home with pieces that you've picked up on your travels or that you've found at a local flea market, you create a deeply personal space that feels incredibly unique.

What comes across instantly as you journey around this home and transition from space to space is an immeasurable sense of warmth, together with its clever fusion of aesthetics. It's a home that feels so very loved. Layered, textural, artisanal, classic, modern, timeless and extremely beautiful – I am obsessed!

Previous pages: A kitchen like no other – from the jaw-dropping, richly veined marble to the beautiful colour on the cabinetry, it's a room that straddles different eras, feeling luxurious and timeless.

Below left: The stunning wallpaper in Oscar's bedroom brings this space to life. Its eye-catching print imbues the room with a great sense of fun and warmth.

Below: The exquisite, unexpected wallcovering in Poppy's bedroom makes her room feel like a fairy tale. This whimsical paper and the beautiful pink tones make it the dreamiest of children's rooms.

# UNLOCKING LIGHTING

What makes a room feel good? The answer is always lighting. It is one of the most poetic and magical creations ever, as it affects how you move through a space, feel and perceive things. It makes or breaks a room. When you get the lighting right, with the flick of a switch you can take a room from average to exceptional. By combining different strengths of light, you can highlight, amplify, create illusion, cast shadow and create depth and intrigue – it's like being a magician.

I find that lighting is so often under-considered, treated as an afterthought. It is super-easy to buy lamps purely because you like them, but you also have to remember that the illumination produced by every single lamp, and every pendant, recessed or wall light, has a huge impact on mood and atmosphere, and can even affect your emotions.

Don't panic though. I don't want you to think you have to hire a lighting designer, because you don't. There are a few ground rules to take into consideration and this chapter will break down the process, enabling you to add depth and character to each room in the house. I've written about how to light rooms in the past, but in this book, I want to take it a step further and talk in detail about creating a tantalizing visual effect.

*A well-planned lighting scheme transforms the way your home looks, feels and even functions. To do that you need a good mix of lights, from the ceiling to the wall to the floor.*

Unlocking lighting

# LAYERED ILLUMINATION: MASTERING THE ART OF MIXING AND MATCHING

*I like wall lights to act as a talking point. Having a showstopper on the wall elevates it no end.*

*I am the hugest fan of plopping lights next to chairs – it creates an instant feature.*

Every room, no matter how big or small, needs a mixture of lighting, from overhead to accent to task. Just to recap, especially if you haven't read my previous books (and why not, may I ask?), lighting is divided into three categories: ambient or general lighting, task lighting, and decorative lighting. There should never be just one form of lighting in a room; variety is fundamental.

*Think about the colour of the light itself when selecting bulbs: warmer hues create a mood perfect for relaxing, evoking a sense of cosiness.*

## Ambient lighting

This is light that suffuses a room with an even glow – it fills in shadows and softens the transition between bright and dark. It's essential for general vision and giving a sense of ease and comfort, yet on its own it's super-dull and flat.

## Task lighting

Focused lighting that illuminates particular areas of activity, such as reading, writing, grooming, cooking and so on, is task lighting. Lamps used for task lighting are often at eye level so that the glaring bulb is never seen. On its own, task lighting creates far too much contrast, so it always needs its buddies – ambient and decorative lighting.

## Decorative lighting

This draws the eye, calling attention to something fabulous like a painting, an architectural feature or a vignette. However, it is far too soft and atmospheric by itself.

There is a reason we layer all three types of lighting together and that is because it instantly lifts the mood. Without getting all deep, when you get the lighting right it enlivens and enriches our senses and thus our lives.

Layers of light are so important – think soft, bold, direct, warm, bright, shimmery, sparkling. I can go on – comforting, welcoming, practical... In a nutshell, what you want is variety. First things first, though. We need to drill down into the orientation of each room.

A foolproof formula is to make sure you have at least one light from each of these three categories. I have far more decorative and accent lighting (small table lamps, string lights and candles) in my living area compared to my bathroom, for example. We'll explore the details of lighting individual rooms later, but as rule, in whatever room we're talking about, you need at least one of each lighting category represented.

*Statement pendants don't necessarily have to be big, they just need to be balanced and catch the eye. Pairing these two pendants over the dining table draws the eye up, and when the eye is drawn up high, you create a beautiful sense of grandeur.*

# CONSIDERING THE ORIENTATION

The direction your home faces affects the amount of light coming in. One orientation is not necessarily better than another, although estate agents in the northern hemisphere like to shout about properties with south-facing windows (while in the southern hemisphere north-facing windows get all the love). The key in creating a successful lighting scheme is to be able to go from morning to evening with lighting that always feels considered and beautiful. I should mention that when you get the lighting right, people will rarely notice. It's like the barista who makes you the perfect cup of coffee – you don't really think about it. When the coffee is bad, you notice.

North-facing rooms receive less direct sunlight, so mix in ambient and task lighting with softer, warmer decorative lighting to create a feeling of instant cosiness.

East-facing rooms will get wonderful warm, yellow light before noon. My house is east–west facing, so in the morning on the east side I rarely have any lights on. As the day progresses and the natural light turns a little bluer, I need artificial light to add pockets of warmth, so I mix in a lot of task and decorative lighting.

South-facing rooms are bathed in warm, flattering light all day long, although this will be harsh at midday when the sun flattens everything out. It's a strong, solid light and it's important on cloudy days, and during the cooler months and evenings, to have a soft lighting scheme that is layered, cosy and atmospheric. Mix your three different categories of light, and remember to pick out lots of accents with decorative lighting.

West-facing rooms have a bluer, cooler light in the mornings, and from noon onwards a warm, soft light with lots of golden overtones. In the earlier part of the day, you'll need to warm things up with a mixture of task and decorative, not forgetting ambient lighting of course.

*A clear glass chandelier near a big window brings a subtle elegance to any room and, as you can see through it, you can afford – as the saying goes – to 'go big or go home'!*

# ESTABLISHING A LIGHTING PLAN

There's no single formula for getting the lighting right as so many factors come into play: from how much natural daylight there is in each room, to how high or low the ceilings are. Aesthetic approaches also differ, so it's about finding the right blend. Ask yourself: how do you use the space? What is its purpose? How do you want the room to feel – cosy, dramatic, playful, sociable or a combo of moods? What do you want to accentuate? Which areas should remain in shadow?

These days, many of our spaces do double duty – for example, dining tables that are used as desks during the day and then in the evening for entertaining. This will require bright ambient and task lighting and also softer accent and decorative light. Many rooms have multiple purposes, which is why when you layer your scheme, you get to create this stimulating visual atmosphere. And no matter how you use it, and how many different aims you need it to achieve, when you layer ambient, task, accent and decorative light, it will never feel flat and boring. You can create so many different looks with how you mix lights.

Always create shadows. I am literally obsessed with shadows and go out of my way to do this purposely and effectively in every room. Shadows provide great depth and intrigue. This effect can be easily achieved by overdosing on table lights, which throw a lovely pool of warm, isolated light downwards, creating an instantly intimate feel; or by opting for narrow beam bulbs in recessed ceilings that give you a really focused, intense light. As odd as this may sound, the best lighting designers in the world also consider themselves to be darkness designers. Figuring out your lighting scheme is not just about brightening a room, it's also about darkening and creating contrast to give the space as much drama and shadow as possible. Shadows emphasize shapes beautifully, so go out of your way to contrast lighting in a subtle, considered way.

Ceilings are easy to light with recessed fixtures, pendants or chandeliers. It's the sides and the middle of rooms that are harder to get right, but so important. Aim to weave the light around and into the room. I get asked a lot about how I'm able to place lights in the middle of my rooms without having sockets in the floor. The answer is super-easy – all my lamps on central coffee tables have a rug underneath. This means I can run the wire down the side of the table and then under and along the rug and off to a switch at the side. Simple, hey?

Moving on to the next and most contentious point – how many lights should there be per room? An average-sized room needs between seven and nine. It sounds like a lot, I know, but it's the only way you will create a magical lighting scheme. We have to think like a lighting designer on a movie set, considering the warmth of the light, the brightness, shapes, shadows, beam angles – it's complex. Uplighting, downlighting, highlighting, marrying practical with aesthetic; you can't achieve that with a small number of lights.

*Above left: For a set of pendants that make a statement, you can't go wrong with a woven material as it lends such a relaxed air to a space.*

*Above: Trade in the typical brass or metal pendant and go for fabric instead. Not only does it add a layer of softness, it also scores high on visual appeal.*

# DIRECT VS INDIRECT

The most successful lighting schemes combine both direct and indirect light.

Direct lighting is all about focused illumination, so a beam of light falls from the fixture onto a specific area. The main goal with this type of lighting is to provide strong illumination for tasks and/or create a bright general lighting plan where there is no diffusion. This can be seen in many forms of overhead lighting and specific task lighting; both downlights and spotlights are great examples. With a powerful beam, direct light can appear quite harsh, so dimmers are key.

Indirect light is where the beam or glow is filtered so there are no sharp contrasts and the light feels warm and welcoming. Wall fixtures, floor and table lamps, as well as pendants crafted from fabric, glass or paper, provide indirect light as the light is filtered through a screen or shade.

Every scheme needs a combination of both types of lighting. If the lighting is all direct it will be too harsh and stark; if it's all indirect it will be too soft and lacking in energy.

*Left: Getting the lighting right in the bedroom is a game changer. Steer clear of one dazzling overhead source of illumination and instead think table lamps, which softly glow and diffuse the light.*

*Opposite: If you want to take a room to another level, concentrate on the detailing. Bedside lamps, beautifully made, add a luxe element while providing focused, direct illumination.*

The best lighting designers in the world also consider themselves to be darkness designers. Figuring out your lighting scheme is not just about brightening a room, it's also about darkening and creating contrast.

# UPSCALING

You can transform any ho-hum room into something cosy, inviting and cocooning by strategically varying the heights of your light sources. It's a trick designers use all the time to create a high-impact space.

In rooms with central hanging fixtures, add as many low lights as you can in different parts of the space, from little table lamps to sconces and candles. This will create the most gorgeous layering effect. Make sure your table lamps are not all at the same height or on the same horizontal plane. If they are, raise some on stacks of books or beautiful storage boxes – this provides interest and instant drama. Constantly ask yourself, have I got the lighting right at floor level, mid-level and ceiling level? I so often find a room that lacks warmth can be transformed with this little trick. Think low lamps everywhere, floor-standing and reading lamps, the odd wall lamp and ceiling lights – layered lighting at its best. The goal is always to create a sense of depth, seducing the eye with highlights and lowlights.

*Right: As any interior designer will tell you, lighting is all about layering – mixing up your light sources so as to diffuse light throughout the whole room. My go-to trick is to elevate any small fixtures by plopping them on a book.*

*Far right: Statement-making pendants add instant grandeur to a space. When you up the scale it draws the eye, and globe-shaped, circular pendants are particularly suited to scaling up.*

Unlocking lighting

# RECESSED LIGHTING

Let's start with recessed lighting. It gets a bit of a bad rap, but I happen to think that in certain rooms it's essential. Recessed lighting will light up areas in a uniform way, making them feel bigger, and it works well in areas where you want to specifically illuminate the edges of the room. Recessed lights take up less space and therefore don't interrupt the visual expanse of the ceiling. They are great in kitchens, bathrooms, home cinemas, home offices, cupboards, hallways, rooms with low ceilings, and rooms with reduced natural light. As they are directional, they brighten and illuminate; without them, food in kitchens will look grey and the upper reaches of shelves and cabinets in home offices and bathrooms will be in darkness.

Recessed light is clear and bright, so don't fall into the trap of overcompensating and putting them everywhere, creating a Swiss cheese effect! But in terms of how many you should use, attitudes are changing. When we installed our recessed lighting years ago, the thinking was all about grid systems, with spots placed at the same distance from one another across the whole ceiling. Nowadays, they are placed in strategic areas – above a kitchen island, for example, or over sinks and workstations.

Beam angle is very important: a spot with a small beam is better suited for accenting an area and drawing your eye over, say, a beautiful sink or bath. In my kitchen I have a narrow beam over a super-large block of wood that acts as my chopping board. This type of beam will make an area sparkle with its clear, directional light. Larger beam angles wash rooms with general light, providing a great sense of illumination.

Trim options are numerous: from metal finishes to fixtures plastered into the ceiling for a seamless look. Bulbs are equally important – I will always love the warmth of incandescent and halogen bulbs, but LEDs are improving. Always go for the warmest LEDs available, making sure they are dimmable, and layer in all other types of lighting for the best look.

*Bathroom lighting not only needs to be practical – it must also help create a stylish sanctuary. The recessed lights behind matching mirrors here, when used without overhead lighting, are a perfect example.*

# TABLE LAMPS

I am obsessed with table lamps; I cannot think of any other finishing touch that simultaneously adds softness, warmth and character. They are such a fabulous decorative tool and can be used to enhance tables, consoles, islands and shelves, providing the most wonderful light.

These lamps are my go-to accessory and my starting point when decorating a table. Use them correctly and they can create symmetry, contrast, colour, scale and texture, not forgetting their main job – illumination.

There's a multitude of styles to choose from: mushroom lamps, rattan lanterns, industrial concrete, arc lamps, tall and slender buffet lamps, tripod, swing arm – the list goes on. From natural materials to contemporary finishes, from wood to alabaster, acrylic, metal, ceramic and glass, the choices are endless. Mix up your styles but make sure not every lamp is a different colour as that can make a room feel a little chaotic. I try to keep my lamps in similar colour families and mix up shapes, materials and styles. Try to avoid buying in twos, à la Noah's Ark – this can look a bit like decorating by numbers and, although it means you have to work a little harder to find cohesion within your collection, your room will feel so much more unique. Table lamps direct the light downwards, which really opens up a space; arrange them all over the room so that your eye moves across the space with ease.

You can reduce the annoyance of plugs and wires by blending them in with your colour palette – I buy dark plugs and wires. You can also have lamps wired with inoffensive clear or fabric cords. Unsightly cables can be tucked or taped to a piece of furniture, and designers often use cable ties to maintain tidiness.

When it comes to shades, the most common types are drum, rectangle and empire, together with the more traditional shapes of bell, pagoda and box pleat. The usual materials are linen, silk, velvet and paper. You'll often find they will have either a metallic or a colour inner, which influences the warmth of the light emitted.

In terms of bulbs, for a warm, soft light go with 2,700 to 3,000K (see page 92 for more on bulbs), otherwise known as warm white. The higher you go up the colour temperature range, the bluer the light becomes, giving you that dreaded hospital/garage look, so keep it low.

*This beautiful table lamp would look as good in a dining room as it would in a bedroom, softly diffusing the light with its woven shade.*

# A CRASH COURSE ON PLACING TABLE LAMPS

## Side tables

Put lamps on every single side table you have: by your bed, next to a sofa or chair, beside a bench. Everywhere!

## Mantelpieces

These are a perfect platform for skinny lamps, and the radiance coming from the light is taken to new heights if you prop a mirror behind them.

## Shelves

Lamps on every shelf, lighting the edges of a room, will add so much softness and make a space feel especially inviting.

## Kitchen counters

Don't neglect these. This one of the most game-changing things you can do, instantly making things cosier. I have two lamps on my central island and three lamps on my benchtop and it's taken the kitchen to a whole new level.

*The beautiful design of this gold table lamp would add a luxurious touch to any space. It's sculptural and sleek in equal measure.*

Unlocking lighting

This is easy because there are hardly any places that lamps can't go! Perfect in hallways and entranceways, and so beautifully warm and welcoming on any table, shelf or console, they lift things no end and add such drama.

*A vintage 1950s Italian table lamp perched on a kitchen island immediately draws the eye and creates great intrigue.*

# FLOOR LAMPS

Floor lamps are generally regarded as the supporting players in a scheme – rarely the star, yet so necessary. Offering up both ambient and direct task lighting, they are super-versatile. They add immediate warmth, and often diffuse light for semi-direct illumination. Semi-translucent shades give softer, ambient light, while opaque shades offer up decorative accent lighting. Floor lamps for reading provide direct, focused light down to an armchair, sofa or bed, and some versions have arms that cantilever out to make this even more targeted and flexible. Taller lamps add a obvious sculptural dimension to a room, so when choosing, pick something for its shape.

Make sure your floor lamps relate in some way to the other lamps in the room, so things feel harmonious. You certainly shouldn't match them – just keep the tones consistent with everything else. Use them in empty areas, such as a gap between a sofa and the wall, or by the side of a window, as they will add instant depth and bring the room to life. When combined with table lamps, desk lamps, pendants and wall lamps, you get this multifaceted, layered look that is flattering, distinctive, characterful and so very beautiful. As a general rule, I wouldn't go for more than two floor lamps in a room, and often I prefer just one.

*Floor lights are often under-considered, yet there is no better way to create instant ambience than a well-placed floor lamp. Use them to highlight corners of a room while also making a serious style statement.*

## Foolproof places for floor lamps

☐ **Beside an armchair or to the side of a sofa** Always looks gorgeous.

☐ **In empty corners** This will help create a uniform lighting scheme.

☐ **In front of a window** A lovely choice as this keeps the light levels up as daylight transitions into dusk.

☐ **In the dining room** A great way to add character and ambience to this socializing/entertaining space.

☐ **Near architectural features or art** Floor lamps are a great tool for highlighting decorative accents.

# PENDANTS AND CHANDELIERS

*This beautiful supersized pendant lends shape and texture to the room. Echoing the materiality on the ceiling, it adds a whole other level of warmth and texture.*

Is there any room that doesn't need a pendant or chandelier? I can't think of one, and all my rooms have them. They direct the eye upwards, and in doing so will make any room feel grander by opening up the space. Suspended alone, in a single cluster or in a circular armature of bulbs, these beautiful accentuation fixtures make rooms look and feel glamorous.

Go as large as you dare for instant drama. Oversized pendants and chandeliers look phenomenal, defining a space. It's known in the biz as playing around with scale, and I am one of its biggest fans. You get this interesting effect when you supersize; it adds tension, and tension in interiors creates magic. There are so many different types, from drum- and dome-shaped pendants to globe, linear, cord and lantern styles – and that's just pendants. With chandeliers you can opt for candle types (the granddaddy of all chandeliers), antler, crystal, futuristic, bowl, beaded, caged and tiered. From traditional to modern, ceramic to glass, there is a great range of styles to choose from. Work out your aesthetic and the vibe you are going for. If, for example, your rooms are lacking texture, opt for fixtures crafted from wood, fabric or ceramic. If you want something more glam, go for glass. Position them everywhere and anywhere: above dining tables (obvious), in hallways, at the top of a staircase, above a kitchen island (moi), in pairs either side of a bed, or even in the bathroom. If your ceilings are low, don't let that put you off – hang them off-centre with a low table beneath. I also think you can be a little risky with where you place them. See below for some ideas.

## Risk-taking places for pendants and chandeliers

- ☐ **Over a kitchen island** I've done this, and it feels so glamorous, creating an instant, dramatic scene.
- ☐ **In the home office** Take the space to a whole new level of sophistication with a pendant or chandelier suspended above the desk.
- ☐ **Off to the side** Hang chandeliers and pendants artfully in nooks, alcoves and little corners – unexpected and beautiful.
- ☐ **In the bedroom** Always. Adding a wow pendant to a bedroom makes the space feel much more special, whether it's above the bed or over a chair.
- ☐ **In the hallway** Pendants and chandeliers are lovely additions to hallways, adding elegance, sophistication and, of course, illumination.
- ☐ **Above a coffee table** This looks fabulous, turning the table into an fabulous focal point and tying the room together.

# WALL LIGHTS

I feel wall lights are a little under-considered, yet they add so much to a layered lighting scheme, providing both ambient, accent and even task lighting. I love them in dark corners as they create a cosy layer, and if ceilings are low and a main ceiling fixture is not a feasible option, they make a fabulous alternative.

I have wall lights in my kitchen and studio, and they provide depth and intrigue with their soft, subtle light, which is perfect for both relaxing and entertaining. You can also use them to highlight an architectural feature or artwork, or plop them either side of an alcove for drama and focus.

You can choose between uplights and downlights. Uplights cast light towards the ceiling, which opens up a room; downlights direct the light in the opposite direction, making for a cosy, relaxing atmosphere. I always opt for downlights.

Wall lights come in all shapes, sizes and styles, with swing arms, sconces, and as reading lights and picture lights, providing stylish and flexible options for every room in the house. When it comes to positioning, it depends on so many things, from the proportions of the room to the size of the fixture, but as a rough guide they should be positioned from around 1.5 to 1.7m (5 to 5½ft) above floor level, the idea being that the top of the wall light sits at eye level. Obviously, if they are going above shelves, they can be placed much higher.

*The sleek design of this wall light (note there is only one) allows for a nuanced mix of light and shade.*

## Transformational spots for wall lights

- □ **In an alcove** Wall lights are perfect for highlighting any alcove or niche with their warm, soft glow.
- □ **In the bedroom** Providing a softer option than the main ceiling light, wall lights are a beautiful feature for bedrooms.
- □ **In the bathroom** Flanking a mirror (very hotel-ish) they create a lovely visual balance.
- □ **In the kitchen** I have mine over a shelf, but they look just as good on either side of a cooker.
- □ **On a landing** Perfect for illuminating small, awkward spaces that would otherwise be ignored.
- □ **In the hallway** Where space is generally limited, a set of wall lights will diffuse the light perfectly, creating a welcoming feeling.

Unlocking lighting

# BULBS: CREATING THE PERFECT GLOW

If I asked you to think about light for a second, my guess is you're probably not picturing white, cold, blue light. More likely it's a warm, golden glow – the kind you get when the sun dips below the horizon, or from the reflected glow of embers in a fire at the end of an evening. Soft, rosy and golden: hold that thought when buying bulbs.

Choosing bulbs is all about colour temperature – how warm the light appears. It's measured on the Kelvin scale (K), and the higher the K value, the bluer or whiter the light. Bulbs vary according to the manufacturer, but as a general guide 2,700 to 3,000K is soft, warm white; bright, cool white is 3,500 to 4,100K; and daylight is 5,000 to 6,000K. If you want to cosy up a room, always use warmer, softer, yellower light; task-orientated areas like bathrooms and kitchens can go a little brighter.

Incandescent bulbs are being phased out (these are my favourite as I love their warm, soft light) as are halogens, which emit a white light simulating high-noon. Thankfully, LEDs have come a long way, with many options to choose from, and exposed filament bulbs are a trend that continues to grow. With their sultry, candle-like glow and beautiful shapes, they're just as fabulous exposed as encased, creating a warm, relaxed vibe.

*Left: With a chandelier, opt for Edison-style bulbs. Their varied shapes add so much interest, and provide the softest of glows.*

*Opposite: These filament incandescent bulbs (reproductions of the Edison bulb) have the warmest glow, making them ideal for use without a shade. There is such power in groupings consisting of an odd number of items, so if possible, stick to odd numbers when suspending lights.*

Unlocking lighting

# LIGHTING IDEAS AROUND THE HOME

Each room in your house has different lighting requirements but nowhere needs to be dull, functional or boring. Be bold, be creative and change things up so every space is lit to perfection.

## LIVING ROOMS

The lighting plan for living rooms must be strategic and multifunctional, enabling us to kick back, work, watch a movie, read or entertain.

As we've already discussed, the most successful schemes combine several light sources at varying levels from myriad fixtures, which can be used together or separately. Sconces are fabulous when walls are empty and you want to create intrigue and wash an area with light. They are also great for highlighting art, accenting an architectural feature or framing a sofa. Pairs of wall lights always draw the eye, look amazing in alcoves and, if your space is small, they are even more fundamental as they free up floor space.

A central pendant or chandelier completes a living room, creating an instant focal point. Anything hanging from the ceiling will need to be dimmable so you can dial the atmosphere up or down and set the mood. Recessed lighting also works if you have very little natural light. Table lamps should be everywhere and anywhere – on shelves, mantels, coffee tables and occasional tables, and beside sofas and chairs. Floor lamps illuminating corners or seating areas will also cast a beautiful soft glow. If your living room is super-spacious, consider dividing up the seating area with two distinct spaces, then create symmetry by suspending two identical fixtures over these areas. Take a cue from some of the coolest hotels – they do this a lot.

*There is no better way to elevate a living room than through lighting. Varying the height of your fixtures by adding wall lights, for example, adds instant verticality. This takes the eye up to the ceiling, which always makes a room appear grander than it really is.*

## BEDROOMS

The right type of lighting is crucial for bedrooms as it needs to be suitable for relaxing, sleeping and reading. Like all other rooms, bedrooms require a fabulous combo of lights, from bedside lamps to ceiling fixtures, floor lamps and sconces, making it easy to wind down. You can save space on your bedside tables if they are small by hanging pendants either side, which is super-hotel-ish. You can also put sconces on the wall behind the bed, creating the perfect backdrop and washing the wall with light.

If you have room for a chair, always place a floor light or little table and a lamp next to it, creating a cosy nook to read and chill. Chandeliers always look fabulous hung centrally, and again, sconces can provide beautiful decorative and task lighting for reading. In my world, bedside lamps should never be matched: it's far more intriguing if you mix things up. Vary the shapes, combining round, oval and square, creating instant visual interest, and use different materials, too. Visual weight is also key for lamps on either side of a bed – they need to relate to each other.

*Left: Using layers of light is fundamental for creating mood. Here, an adjustable wall sconce provides task lighting or ambient light as required.*

*Opposite: Everyone's fave natural material, rattan, works beautifully in a bedroom lighting scheme. This tremendously textured pendant adds instant character.*

97

## KITCHENS

Kitchens are the engine room of any home and the most frequently used, so the lighting has to be both practical and functional, as well as intriguing, tantalizing and exciting – quite a big ask! This room requires myriad light sources of different types to create an inviting atmosphere.

I often think people go wrong with kitchen lighting by keeping it too functional. Single pendants or grids of recessed lighting create glare and are unflattering, so we need other light sources to help out.

Anything in or hanging from the ceiling must be on dimmers. This allows us to control the light levels and dial light up when prepping and cooking, and dial it down for a more intimate atmosphere. I happen to think that all kitchens need a pendant or chandelier as it adds softness to such a practical space, bringing an unexpected note while embellishing with its immediate visual interest.

Task lighting is essential and can be provided by table lamps, floor lamps or ceiling lights. It is essential for countertops, islands, sinks and above cabinets. Never neglect accent and decorative lighting in kitchens. I plonk little table lamps everywhere; these add softness and transform what is a practical space into a room that you never want to leave.

## BATHROOMS

Bathrooms are one of the hardest rooms to light as they are often small, with limited natural light, and have fewer outlets and more moisture to contend with. It's incredibly important to counterbalance these shortcomings by getting clever with the lighting.

Lighting for bathrooms needs to be both energizing and bright to help wake you up and get ready for the day, and soft, spa-like and relaxing to help you unwind in the evening.

General ambient light is fundamental and typically comes from recessed lights – just try and avoid laying them out in a regular grid formation. Instead, place them over the sink or bath, or highlight a wall, towel rail or feature. Chandeliers are great if your ceilings are high enough, but don't rely on the light, as without its buddies it will be too flat. And remember that the fitting must be IP (Ingress Protection) rated so that it's safe for use near water.

Wall-mounted lights can add concentrated task lighting around sinks and vanities for dental care, shaving, make-up and so forth, as well as beautiful accent lighting. You can add table lamps if they are battery-operated; I have mine on top of cabinets, on a little stool next to the bath and bedside the basin.

Unlocking lighting

*Above left: A lesson in clever styling – the woven pendants echo the materiality of the baskets, so everything feels beautifully cohesive.*

*Above: A veritable design classic, this wall lamp with its sophisticated vibe has real personality. The carbon filament blub adds a further chic charm, not to mention a warm relaxed glow.*

*Below: Elegant and luminous, these contemporary pendants suspended over a table add instant drama.*

*Below right: A glossy black table lamp adds an undeniably chic element to this room. When in use, it will bounce the light around and elevate the space.*

Unlocking lighting

## DINING ROOMS

The lighting in dining rooms should beckon you in, encourage you to linger and feel incredibly relaxing. As we use these spaces a lot more in the evenings, we need to think a little differently about the lighting. I like to keep the lighting in my dining room low and warm, like a fabulous restaurant would, with lots of points of light. I overdose on table lamps as they make the room feel sparkling and special, creating a relaxed atmosphere.

I like to base the lighting scheme around the table, with the rest of the lighting in the room taking a step back and receding. To do this, suspend a chandelier or pendant over the table, hanging it lower than you usually would, and make sure the fitting is on a dimmer to create an intimate atmosphere that's perfect for entertaining. Remember, the bigger the fixture, the better – this will add far more drama to the scheme.

Next, dot table lamps around the perimeter of the room – on sideboards, shelves and occasional tables – so they highlight lovely objects like flowers and books. Accompany them with the odd sconce on the walls to highlight an area or bring attention to an artwork.

## HOME OFFICES

No matter where your home office is located, it's important for it to feel not just functional, but also wonderfully atmospheric. I spend so much time in mine that I want and need it to inspire, put me at ease and be a joy to work in. I also need it to feel just as beautifully lit as any other room in the house.

Mix up the ceiling lighting – recessed and overhead pendants will always work. You don't want to feel drowsy, so the lighting, while all dimmable, must be clear and bright, otherwise you will feel demotivated. It's also important to make sure the whole room is lit properly, not just the work area. Task lighting next to computers and on the worktable is essential. On my desk I have one task light near the computer and two large decorative lights at either end.

When it comes to the rest of the room, make little pockets glow, like reading nooks and shelves; it's just as important to have seductive areas in a room as it is to have functional, well-lit areas. It is called playing with tension, which is fundamental for every room in the house.

## HALLWAYS

Lighting for hallways is often overlooked, and yet it's so important – it's the entry point into your world, so it needs to brighten and welcome simultaneously. In the daytime, on a practical, day-to-day level, anything in the ceiling will give good illumination, whether that's a row of seamless ceiling lights or a pendant. However, it is a little flat on its own, so table lamps are a must as they add an instant glow and atmosphere. For hallways tight on space, consider wall lights, which offer far more versatility and add both warmth and texture.

# JASON ATHERTON
## A lighting masterclass

Throughout, the most incredibly soft, cinematic lighting casts sultry pools of light, giving each room a wonderful depth.

Unlocking lighting

*The yellow of the upholstery and the lights' glow, offset by a darker background, delight the senses.*

When you step into Jason Atherton's London home you feel like you've walked into one of his beautifully designed, artfully curated restaurants. It was designed by multidisciplinary studio Rosendale Design, which has worked on many of Atherton's restaurants, and their moody approach takes his home space to a whole new level of cool. A warm material and colour palette dominates the scheme. With a focus on the kitchen area – including the most phenomenal dark-stained oak cabinets, along with rainforest-brown marble for the worktops and splashback, not to mention the covetable kitchen island – this family home feels refined, luxurious and incredibly warm.

*The kitchen features dramatic dark cabinetry and splashbacks, while the corner banquette and table give a sense of being in one of Jason's beautifully designed restaurants.*

Unlocking lighting

Unlocking lighting

Atmospheric, luxurious and deeply relaxing, this is a space that encourages you to linger. The kitchen, for example, is bordered by a curved leather booth at one end, providing a cosy communal dining area that feels incredibly intimate yet remains beautifully connected to the cooking area. The sophistication of the design then continues with a games room, wine cellar and even a cinema.

The house has its own distinctive personality, combining refinement with cosiness, and paying homage to tradition while remaining utterly contemporary. Luxurious textiles like butter-soft leather are featured alongside eclectic artwork,

and throughout, the most incredibly soft, cinematic lighting casts sultry pools of light, giving each room a wonderful depth. It's a home that manages to be cutting-edge cool and charismatic at the same time.

Craftsmanship and attention to detail shine throughout, from the wonderful wood panelling in the games room, to the thoughtful use of materials in the bathrooms, kitchen, living spaces and even the walk-in wardrobes. Bespoke cabinetry runs throughout, alongside pieces of furniture crafted by a network of artists and artisans, all of whom have contributed to creating a house that boasts unbelievable style.

*Opposite: The games room is a visual beacon of colour, with a lighting scheme that provides both illumination and drama.*

*Below: An inky palette combined with subtle lighting produces instant refinement.*

*Overleaf: The perfect atmosphere has been created in the dining room, with a richly layered lighting scheme and the softest palette on the walls. Reflective surfaces enhance the brightness, with the materials used throughout being of superb quality.*

WALL WISDOM

I read this somewhere not so long ago: 'What is your home if not a place to collect memories?' It was such a lovely way of thinking, and what better place to display and create memories than by beautifying your walls? Being one of the largest areas of a room, it is vital to choose the right treatment, so look upon your walls as the perfect canvas for adding your own unique narrative.

In this chapter we will explore gallery walls, as well as creative and imaginative ways to hang things on them, from baskets to rugs, but for now let's concentrate on wall coverings and how to select what's right. Before determining which treatment to apply, like paint, wood or wallpaper, you need to figure out your style aesthetic. Do you want bold walls that make a statement, or something that recedes and is easier to live with?

If you prefer a pared-back look, then a textured wall covering or limewash paint will look amazing and add instant visual interest. If you are planning a gallery wall, then a heavily patterned wallpaper will compete and appear too busy, as will a really daring, strong paint colour. There are endless ways to spice up your walls, from painting them in the most luxurious of hues, to thinking outside the solid-hued box and covering them with the most phenomenal, printed wallpaper. Look upon walls as the perfect place to write your story by giving guests a little insight into who you are. You can then embellish them with art, mirrors, shelving or wall hangings. You can add in a statement-making accent wall, hang a rug, embrace macramé, include storage or go for a salon-style installation of wall baskets.

Wall treatments and wall décor can go beyond our wildest dreams. It can feel intimidating, but don't be afraid to experiment. While there is nothing wrong with an empty wall, if *all* your walls are empty, things are going to feel super-flat.

*Plastered walls are having a moment, with the warmth and texture of their muted palette taking any room from ordinary to totally extraordinary.*

Wall wisdom

What you decide to put on your walls will have the most enormous effect on a room's atmosphere, since walls occupy so much visual space. It's a powerful thing to know that what you put on your walls can make a room feel calming, invigorating or energizing – all because of your choice of wall treatment.

For example, I have an earthy mid- to dark-tone paint palette throughout my home. I find I relax easily into these soft, cocooning hues. I draw inspiration for my palette from countries in warmer latitudes and the infinitely rich colours of the earth. Baked clays, browns, olives, rich greens, pinky browns and caramels are my preferred tones. They are calming in the bedroom, restorative in the living room and grounding in the hallway. Other people might plump for lighter or brighter hues. There isn't a wrong or a right; so much of it has to do with your personality and how you want your home to feel. I need my home to optimize relaxation since my days are so full-on, so I decorate my walls with colours or materials that promote restfulness. From the most calming of plaster wall coverings in my bathroom (tadelakt) to wood-clad walls in the bedroom – they are treatments that don't overtake conversations, making it easy for me to unwind.

Wall wisdom

*Cladding walls in wood has been around for centuries and it will never go out of fashion; it works seamlessly with any style, adding oodles of texture and intrigue.*

# CREATING COHESION

When planning wall colours and treatments for the most sophisticated of schemes, make things as harmonious as you can, and look upon the place as a whole. I know having to establish a colour scheme for a whole house sounds daunting, but the coolest designers around the world do this routinely, as it creates the most cohesive of homes. Rooms flow seamlessly as you transition from space to space; whether this is through a colour connection or materiality, there is visual continuity. The trick is to give each room its own colour personality while ensuring a united look. A one-colour look running throughout reads as incredibly dull, and although it's easy to do, I would avoid it at all costs. An easy way to add varying hues to different rooms is to use a similar group of colours, like my warmer-latitude shades, for instance. This will create that all-important colour continuity, as well as diversity, which is equally important.

You can also invert colours between rooms, which always looks beautiful. For example, in my open-plan lower ground floor, I have a caramel sofa and inky dark walls, and in the kitchen, there are caramel cabinets and inky accessories, so I am switching the dominant colour in these two spaces. The trick is to match the tonality between rooms as much as you can, and by this I mean go for shades with the same strength, regardless of their colour. Using a family of colours in combination always works and I've done this throughout. I've then opted for graduated tones in different strengths from the same pigments in the accessories and soft furnishings, which provides a seamless colour journey.

*Right: Creating a cohesive palette of colours between the walls and other materials throughout your home creates such a relaxed, calm atmosphere.*

*Far right: Dividing walls in half using colour isn't for the faint-hearted. The trick, as always, is to repeat those colours elsewhere throughout the space.*

When you add in further unifying elements, such as all shelving and built-ins being in the same material or colour, you will increase continuity and flow even more. Working with a streamlined palette not only brings instant cohesion, it also helps with the transitions between rooms. I find it's hugely comforting when each room complements the next, as there is instantly greater fluidity, and it creates a more grounding environment in which to nest.

Colour preferences are so personal, and rest assured there is no one correct palette. If you love neutrals because they make you feel calm and secure, then go for neutrals; if you like earthier, deep hues because they make you feel more grounded, connected and restored, plump for them. Creating a cohesive palette isn't that hard to do. I would suggest always starting with the main connector: the hallway. It's so often neglected, but a hallway (and stairs) runs throughout a home, with all other rooms leading off it; it also acts as the entry point into your world.

For example, in my hallway I have a muddy brown hue, while the rooms leading off it are a pinky brown and a browny black – brown being the underlying unifying hue. I think of my home as one big palette rather than lots of individual little rooms. I always keep the colour of the skirting boards, window frames, ceilings and doors consistent with the colour on the walls, and then I continually repeat accessory colours from room to room.

Of course, not all rooms have to flow harmoniously, especially if they are not included in a particular sightline, so loos, home offices and bedrooms, for example, can be different. My preference, though, is for them to blend seamlessly.

*Left: The built-in around this bed is a clever way of adding intrigue and storage at the same time, and it blends harmoniously with the pinky-browny palette.*

*Opposite: Exposed brick walls add instant warmth and texture and are great in transitional walk-through spaces like hallways and landings. When you apply texture to walls, things always look and feel more interesting.*

# LIGHT WALLS VS DARK WALLS

*Above: Saturated, moody walls are my idea of heaven. Wonderfully cocooning, these richer hues add instant drama.*

*Opposite: The colour you apply to your walls has an immediate effect on your emotions. Opting for calming, chalky tones creates a gentle background that is both comforting and easy on the eye.*

Whatever camp you're in (and you already know mine), figuring out the palette for your walls isn't easy. Some of us feel happiest in neutral schemes and others prefer a little colour. I would say that 70 per cent of the examples I see in magazines, on blogs and around my neighbourhood are all-white interiors. It's an astounding trend that zillions of people have adopted around the globe. It's been celebrated across continents, and that's because pale schemes are so easy to live with; the look is clean and classic, and whether your design aesthetic is minimalist, boho or glam, it totally works. I think that's the key to the longevity of this palette – it can be translated to any kind of space, anywhere in the world. It looks just as beautiful in living rooms with soft paper lights and woven rugs as it does when complementing appliances in kitchens. It's classic and chic in bedrooms, stylish and tranquil in bathrooms, and it's practical in hallways and home offices – it makes a space feel immediately refined.

Vanillas, fluffy summer-cloud creams, calicos, off-whites, blush tones and greys: dozens of colours fall under the light umbrella and absolutely go beyond beige. They are the perfect backdrop to build upon and will never overwhelm the eye with too many tones. It's also much easier to change the look of rooms by keeping the colour palette on the walls as neutral as you can, and then adding intrigue with artworks, cushions and accessories; it's also far less expensive than constantly repainting. The trick is to introduce a variety of tones and textures, such as woods, metals and clays, to keep things lively and interesting, and to create depth.

To take things to the next level, always consider the purpose of a particular space. Kitchens and home offices, for example, work with cooler neutrals as those shades create a bright atmosphere in which to work, whereas bedrooms and living rooms are better suited to warmer neutrals with a yellower or pinkier base.

Pale schemes are so easy to live with; whether your aesthetic is minimalist, boho or glam, it totally works.

# PIGMENTED PALETTES

Pigmented palettes have found their way into interiors on all media platforms, and as much as I hate the phrase, they are very on-trend. Many paint brands have recently named a darker, more intense shade their colour of the year! Moody, inky, deeply complex, sophisticated and intense, these hues will always make spaces feel more comforting and cocooning. If used on all four walls, ceilings, skirtings and trim, they also perform this incredible visual trick of making a room feel bigger. This is because you lose the detail – things merge and therefore become less obvious. When corners go into shadow, as they do with darker shades, you get to create this mysterious vibe; you can't actually read where the room ends, so it appears larger.

*Used for centuries in Morocco, tadelakt is a waterproof material that looks just like limewash or plaster. Undeniably eye-catching, its smooth, continuous surface is so beautiful in bathrooms.*

While blush, white and paler hues will always reign supreme in many people's homes, I do think the tide is shifting as we crave more grounding colours that promote calmness – I know I do. I think another reason they are gaining traction is because they generally pair so beautifully with many different palettes.

From rich browns to gauzy soft caramels, sea foam greens to muddy, pinky browns, these earthy hues are deeply saturated, and are able to connect you to the outside and relax you at the same time. Moody, dark hues add coolness to rooms, making them dramatic, but just remember a few tricks of the trade. Always include neutral accents – they will pop and brighten the darker walls. Add in as many reflective elements as you dare, such as mirrors and highly reflective bowls, trays and chair legs. And natural materials will keep things from feeling too stark by adding a large dose of cosiness.

*Opposite: If your palette isn't that pigmented a beautiful option to add variation, depth and intrigue is to go for a finish that has natural variation, such as plaster, tadelakt, lime plaster or concrete.*

*Right: Swoon-worthy tadelakt on the wall, with its absence of grout lines and soft interplay of different colourations, keeps your eye moving through the space.*

Wall wisdom

# BORED WITH PLASTER?

You can add charm, create depth and character and avoid coolness on your walls with many options other than plaster. Take panelling, for instance: this is a great way to add warmth and interest to rooms. Architects and designers love plywood for its natural beauty; it's also strong, lightweight and relatively inexpensive. Other modern panelling options that look and feel super-chic are natural oak, walnut, responsibly sourced veneer, and ornate ribbed and portrait panels. You can tap into the rustic vibe with earthy planks, evoking a cabin feel, or go more boho with cane webbing panels.

*Opposite: Expansive and dramatic, full-height panelled walls add instant charisma to any space, and with so much texture you can pretty much leave them unadorned.*

*Right: Walls are given an extra dimension when plywood is applied; its subtle grain adds a lovely decorative embellishment.*

You can create an instant period style with moulded wainscoting wall panels; go for a large-scale grid for a nod to history. If you fancy going a little more coastal, opt for tongue and groove; for something a tad more relaxed, then Shaker-style panels are the answer. There are many ways to add charm, cosify and create grandeur for every wall in the house.

All rooms need a jumping-off point – something that sets the tone and makes them feel more pulled together. Wallpapering one wall, a ceiling or all the walls creates such impact that, believe it or not, it makes a room easier to design because you already have the texture, pattern, motif or colour to lead off from. It is a great way to breathe new life into a space, from eye-catching florals to stripes and seagrass. For any commitment-phobes out there, fear not, there are also many removable wallpaper options. Otherwise known as peel and stick, this is a great choice if you're scared to commit or live in a rented home.

Mural papers are great as they don't have an identical repeat; they feel super-bespoke, demand attention and are often used on accent walls. The latest in printing technology has taken photo-realism to a whole new level, so you can find wonderful, realistic textures like wood, stone and concrete, or papers featuring forests, cityscapes, landscapes or the ocean, which create a unique look.

There is no denying the power of wallpaper – it instantly upgrades any master bedroom, dining room, living room or accent wall. You can go dainty and subtle, or high impact and bold, and you can choose to sheathe your walls in anything from starbursts to mosaics, palms, geometrics and animal motifs, and from Japanese silk-screened papers to grasscloth. A tried-and-tested trick many designers use is to save boldly printed and highly pigmented papers for behind sofas, beds or desks. This way, you can appreciate the paper when you walk through the door, but it's not in your line of vision while you're in the room, distracting you. Pattern has a significant effect and any print with movement is by far the easiest way to invigorate a wall. A large print will always make a room look and feel more important; smaller rooms will appear more impressive and larger rooms will seem more intimate. A fail-safe way to add pizazz is always to think about the way the pattern runs. For instance, horizontal patterns make rooms feel bigger, while verticals make a room feel taller; diagonal patterns add more movement and rhythm, and small patterns add depth and texture.

I think any room can benefit from wallpaper; it brings dimension to even the smallest of spaces. In the home office you can be quite daring with the print, while in the bedroom I would go subtle with texture. Statement walls, and more specifically, fabric-covered walls, add so much sophistication to a room, quickly transforming it. From seagrass to paisley fabric wallpaper, these treatments add luxury and warmth to any home. Textile wall coverings are textured wallpapers made from natural fibres and man-made yarns, such as silk, linen, banana fibre, coconut bark and braided banana bark, and these all create interesting surface finishes.

*The most dramatic way to change up your home is to elevate your walls. When you upholster them like this, the feeling is luxurious and opulent, reminiscent of a boutique hotel.*

*Providing natural tactility with the use of beautiful tiles enhances this kitchen, giving its walls depth and intrigue.*

# CREATIVE WAYS TO TAKE CEILINGS TO NEW HEIGHTS

A ceiling covers such a large expanse that the shade you paint it has a big impact on the overall mood. It's important, therefore, to consider whether you want to make it stand out or recede.

Darker, lighter, the same colour – a painted ceiling offers an incredible way to spice up your interior. There's no rule that says ceilings should be white, and there are so many other creative options out there.

For years now I have been painting my ceilings the same colour as my walls, for many reasons: it draws the eye up, and therefore creates the illusion of a larger room; it accentuates high ceilings; and it makes rooms with lower ceilings appear both taller and larger. It is also stylish, super-modern and very flattering.

There are other options, of course, but when choosing the right colour for your ceiling, drill down into what the room is used for. For example, warm oranges and pinks make skin tones appear bright, so they are fabulous for bathrooms and social spaces. Blue goes anywhere, while greens can make the skin appear cool, so may not be ideal for bathrooms and bedrooms. You can also texturize a ceiling with a paper or print, add accent beams, wood panels, plump for a coffered ceiling, add tiles, a mural, contrast the paint colour, go glossy – I could go on and on. The ceiling is a real opportunity to flex your decorating muscles. Known as the fifth wall, a ceiling can jazz up any room by adding a totally unique focal, or it can recede like mine do and make your room appear grander, larger and cooler – all because you've painted it in the same colour as the rest of the room!

Think of the ceiling as the fifth wall. A creative
ceiling can completely change the look and feel
of the space.

Panelling a ceiling in wood draws attention
without being overwhelming, adding a
beautifully organic vibe to a space.

Wall wisdom

Wall wisdom

The reason I'm obsessed with interiors is because there are so many variables; if the one wash of colour over the entire room isn't your thing, you could have a darker ceiling. It will cosy up the room immediately, automatically making it seem more inviting and cool. Just be careful with low ceilings: going dark with lighter walls will make a room feel claustrophobic because the ceiling will appear lower. You can also paint the ceiling lighter than your walls, which is the most common ceiling/wall combo out there. It's a formula that's safe, but with so many other options available I would be tempted to dabble. And, if you've never tried it, do give painting out the ceiling the same colour as the walls a go – it's a game-changer and one of the most transformational things you can do.

In terms of finishes I am a fan of matt paint; due to its lack of sheen it reflects less light. The more gloss in a paint, the more it will reflect the light, and glossy ceilings show up every blemish and crack, so make sure they are in perfect condition before applying.

*Far left: A ceiling painted in a paler tone works when there is not too much contrast with the wall colour, as it feels more seamless and cosy.*

*Left: When you paint the ceiling the same colour as walls, it will draw the eye up, creating the illusion of a much larger room.*

# THE DOS AND DON'TS OF THE ACCENT FEATURE WALL

Accent walls have been a huge subject of debate, and for quite some time now they've been considered very uncool! There is a lot of snootiness around them – I think because they are often done in a random colour that doesn't relate to the rest of the room. An accent wall can feel like a bit of a lazy approach, and if you're not careful, it can make a room look unfinished. However, ignore all that and embrace them – they are fabulous for differentiating zones, highlighting architectural features and adding intrigue to awkward corners.

It's super-important that an accent wall relates to the rest of the room, so if you happen to paint out a fireplace, an alcove or the end wall of a landing in a cool colour, make sure you echo that colour back in your accessories and other finishing touches. This will have the effect of making the contrast between the accent wall and the rest of your room less jarring, so the scheme will automatically feel more balanced.

The fab thing about feature walls is that they help distinguish an area and carve out a portion of a room in a cool way, so you can use them to define a room creatively – without having to put up actual walls. They are great for highlighting fireplaces, mouldings and other architectural features, and they don't need to be limited to walls. Painting out doors, bookcases, built-ins and cabinetry will also help draw the eye. I happen to think accent walls work well in hallways or on landings, as both these spaces are often overlooked decoratively, and using a warm, welcoming colour will create the loveliest of impressions. Go dark at the end of a long corridor to make the space feel more elongated, or go bold on the back of the front door, which is super-quirky; you could even add some character and paper one wall to notch up the intrigue. You can go for a dramatic contrast; neutral and soft, perhaps picking up a tone that's lighter or darker than the other three walls in the room; or you can add texture through materiality. Brick, wood, tadelakt, concrete and grasscloth all look beautiful on accent walls.

Choosing which wall to accent is best decided by the effect you want. It might be a chimney breast, headboard, architectural feature or simply a wall behind a TV or sofa that you want to highlight for contrast. You shouldn't have more than one accent wall in a room, though, or it will lose its impact; the whole point is to create a decorative highlight. You want it to be the star of the show.

*When it comes to an accent wall, think beyond paint and instead consider covering it with a texture like this beautiful wood – it will always work!*

# GALLERY WALLS, PICTURES AND EPHEMERA

I love a good gallery wall as it is such a personal way to enhance a space; cladding a wall with a curated mix of art is a wonderful opportunity to express your personality. From sketches to old photos, graphic prints, shots from your phone, kids' art and postcards, gallery walls offer the chance to add a big dollop of creative flair. I don't think they will ever go out of style. They can seem a little bit daunting at first, so before you whack a load of holes in your wall, grab some newspaper or children's art paper, tape it together and spread it out on the floor, then place your pictures within that area until you have the arrangement and the effect you want.

There are some rules; they are not hard and fast, mind you, so feel free to break them if you want to.

Start with the biggest piece in the collection and try and keep it away from the centre. It can go off-centre or in one of the corners; this makes the arrangement far less predictable, stimulates the eye and makes it travel around the wall more. Another great tip is to place the second largest piece on a diagonal from the largest piece, then you just need to fill in the empty spaces in between. You will also need a good combo of vertical and horizontal pieces to keep things interesting. Don't worry about sticking to one style of frame: white, black, wood, ornate gold – all of these will work. I would just advise against having every frame a different style; if you have two or three the same, the wall will feel more considered. Generally speaking, but by no means set in stone: thin black or white frames lend a contemporary edge and work with all posters and photography; ornate gilded frames are taken to another level when the artwork within them is abstract – it adds that little bit of tension and glamour into the mix; and wooden frames add warmth.

*An accent wall in a paper works best when you take into account the other colours in the room, harmoniously linking the palette – as seen here, with the mirrors and soft furnishings picking up on the grounding shade of the paper.*

Of course, not everything needs a frame. I often hang art or prints using bulldog clips, then I will add in a basket or wall sconce to break up the grid-like pattern of the art wall. I think it is a nice touch to have the odd unframed piece or different object as it feels less cookie-cutter and more like it has been curated over time. I also like to rein in the colour palette within the collection so that the tones and intensity of the art always feel sophisticated and considered.

A grid layout is not the only option, either. You can incline the gallery wall up and along a staircase, and even opt for a leaning combo on a sideboard or shelf. Casual, leaning displays with varied heights create beautiful vignettes against walls, and you don't have to nail everything in.

I know it can feel quite intimidating, but no matter what the configuration, scale and orientation of your gallery wall, if you plump for a definite colour palette you can never go wrong. I also like to throw in contrasting shapes or objects like circles or ovals to soften all those angles. You don't have to be predictable, either: a small grouping of art above a doorway is unexpected and makes you look up.

Shelves on walls with a sprinkling of art propped up also read as super-cool, especially if you pepper in small objects like sculpture or foraged finds. I often frame tear sheets from magazines or postcards and like mixing in these fab cheap little items with more special pieces. Both give me joy!

*Open shelving has immense aesthetic appeal. Creating a large-scale statement feature wall, it also merges function with decoration.*

Wall wisdom

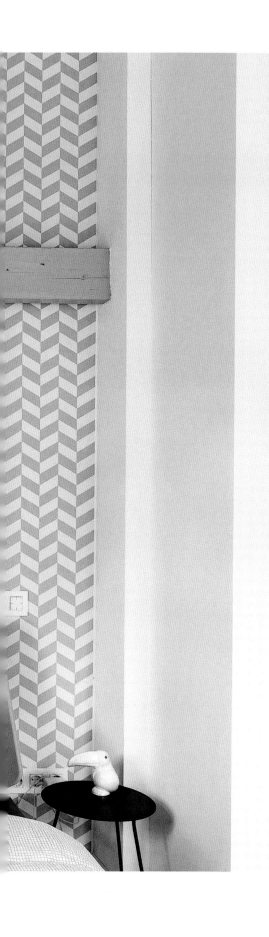

# FANCIFYING WALLS

Bringing empty walls to life with things other than pictures is so easy and transformative. It doesn't matter if you live in a city or in the country, whether you are a maximalist or a minimalist, if all walls are blank and bare it feels boring. Aside from art there are many other options; my collection of woven baskets and feathered wall hangings adorns landings, hallways and bathrooms, and the pieces add so much texture. A wall hanging or a beautiful textile will look phenomenal simply suspended on a wall, as do mirrors, which reflect light and create depth. Not only that – they instantly make a space feel bigger and brighter and add intrigue. You can also tap into the macramé trend as these wonderful weaves add dimension to walls, and if you want to add visual interest to bare walls, consider a stencilled border, some strategically placed sculpture, bookshelves or even a curtained look! A draped curtain over a blank wall feels super-cosy and adds texture and comfort to any room.

As most hallways and landings are too narrow for furniture, focus on animating your walls with some of these incredible treatments. Whether that's through the coolest of colours or a gorgeous printed wallpaper, some panelling or art and textiles, you can add so much more depth. It's easy to make a hallway a tactile, multidimensional space in which to greet and welcome guests into your home by creating visual interest on your walls. That goes for every single room in the house – adding impact to your walls through colour, materiality and embellishments is one of the most exciting things you can do.

*One of the most stylish ways to dress walls and add interest is through wallpaper. When you are bold with pattern and colour, magic happens.*

# REMEDIES FOR RENTERS

*A funky supersized artwork not only stamps personality on a wall; you can also take it with you from place to place.*

*Portable wall hangings are great if you're renting. Rugs are amazing on walls, especially above a bed.*

You can totally stamp your personality on a rented apartment or house by using some clever portable ideas that won't damage the walls – from the numerous peel-and-stick papers I mentioned on page 130, to rugs and heavy fabrics, which add instant warmth. There are also woven baskets, feathered wall hangings and washi tape, which can be used to create lovely graphic designs. You can also supersize pendants (I do this a lot with fabric and paper lampshades as they take up a lot of visual weight and you see less of the wall), and add mirrors and big artworks. All of these removable additions are perfect for injecting some personality without upsetting your landlord.

*Decorating walls when you rent can be rather challenging. The easiest trick is to de-emphasize the wall by upgrading your accessories so your eye is immediately drawn to them.*

# MANDY LEE
## Warm and welcoming

*The plastered walls and ceiling add such softness to this space, turning it into a calming breath of fresh air, away from the hustle and bustle of the busy Hong Kong streets below.*

Wall wisdom

From the warm, distressed wood to the aged materials, the furnishings and fittings used in the apartment have an inviting, welcoming effect that puts you instantly at ease.

Mandy Lee's stunning apartment is a haven from the bustling city streets of Hong Kong. This serene apartment is a complete contrast to the rich tapestry of life going on below in one of the world's most densely populated metropolises.

With plastered walls running throughout the entire home, adding an element of softness, coupled with a grounding palette, it's a space that feels wonderfully restorative. A clever touch is the lime plaster, which is carried through to the ceilings: not only does this create the illusion of larger rooms, it also draws the eye upwards, making the space feel far grander. Each room seems magical, designed to create an incredible sense of enveloping drama. With its cocoon-like atmosphere, soft colour tones and wonderful use of wood, you just want to hunker down and hang out here.

*Soft curtains, textural walls and gentle colours make Mandy's living room feel super-restorative.*

Wall wisdom

In the dining area, the beautiful panelled wall is actually made from ply, stained an intoxicating dark shade to create a luxurious feel. The furnishings, like the banquette and chairs, have been sourced from all over China, and there is a lot of vintage décor throughout: gorgeous collections of ceramics enliven sideboards, brass accents add sophistication, and woven pieces bring visual warmth and individuality to many of the rooms.

A softly draped curtain separates the kitchen from the open-plan living area, and this nook is finished in a bold, super-moody green. The effect is a lavish-looking space, due to the pots and cookware standing out impactfully against the dark hue.

From the warm, distressed wood to the aged materials, the furnishings and fittings used in the apartment have an inviting, welcoming effect that puts you instantly at ease, while also adding a level of intrigue that is so compelling. The soft/hard contrast between materials takes things to a whole new level and gives this home a truly cohesive feel.

*Below left: A custom-stained plywood wall separates the rooms and gives the dining area a rich, grounded vibe.*

*Centre: The textural plastered finish on the bathroom walls, along with the sophisticated brass accents, are softened with basketry, a vintage wooden stool and a custom-made shower curtain.*

*Below and overleaf: The grounding palette takes an unexpected turn in the kitchen, with its deeply saturated inky green walls contrasting with the paler walls elsewhere. This dramatic room is balanced out with neutral accessories in layers of soothing textures.*

# THE LOW-DOWN
# ON FLOORS

Picking flooring is something everyone agonizes over, and it comes down to more than just taste. Footfall, areas of use, how long you intend to live in your home – all these factors come into consideration. Never mind all the other questions, such as: should the flooring be the same throughout or varied? How do I make new flooring coexist with old flooring? How can I tie everything together? Do rustic planks go with plush carpet? Does vinyl work with wool? There are just so many options to choose between.

There really isn't a wrong or right answer when it comes to options; let's just say there are guidelines. With a floor being the surface we interact with more than any other, it's the most important one in the home, and therefore crucial to get right.

You can vary the floor treatments from room to room, or you can seamlessly integrate for a clean, continuous appearance. Alternatively, you can co-ordinate with similar but slightly different treatments. I always make sure there is some connection between materiality, pattern, colour and shape. Flooring is one of your largest investments and something you are going to live with for quite some time. I happen to think it is one of the hardest home purchases to make, because there are so many choices in terms of dimensions and materials, not to mention care and maintenance issues and price options!

*Black and other darker colours make such a dramatic statement when they're used for staircases, and they contrast beautifully with a paler floor below.*

Although it may not be the first thing to grab our attention when we walk into a room, if you get the flooring wrong, everything can feel off. No matter how much attention you pay to the accessories and the finishing touches, if the bones of a room aren't thoughtfully designed, it may never look exactly right. Flooring is one of decorating's most important decisions: it is the foundation point, both literally and visually, for everything else. Every view and piece you place in a room will be affected by what's underneath, so look upon your floors as the base upon which all other decorating decisions are made.

Whether you swap out, revamp or modify, changing your floors alters the whole scheme. The question is, what type of flooring do you choose? Hardwood, engineered wood, laminate, parquet, painted boards, clay blocks, rugs, carpets – so much time is spent deliberating over the perfect surface: from warm, homely and understated, to glossy and super-glam; from vinyl that replicates earthy wood, stone and concrete, to the most beautiful boards and tiles made from ceramic and porcelain.

As one of the largest elements in every room in the house, the flooring you choose should very much depend not only on your budget but also how you will use each room. The three factors you must always consider are pattern, texture and colour. Unsurprisingly, grey is the most popular colour for floors – it's an easy neutral that works with any style. Dark floors are also lovely as they can feel cosy and sophisticated, while light floors make rooms feel airy.

Before drilling down into all the different options, let's talk matching vs co-ordinating flooring.

*Right: Grey tones work beautifully for floors – their neutrality and calmness are excellent for creating a serene space.*

*Far right: When it comes to flooring, it's important to select a material that reflects your personal style. This wooden flooring adds a very relaxed tone, immediately echoing the furnishings.*

# CRACKING THE CODE ON MIXING AND MATCHING

Should the flooring be the same throughout? This is actually quite a tough question because, as I said before, there really isn't a right or wrong answer. However, if you mix too many flooring types together you can overdo things and that will overpower the space, and if you underplay it, everything can look a little boring.

In open-plan rooms I would absolutely recommend having the same flooring throughout, as it will make your home feel more spacious. Generally, you don't want to have a transition in flooring in open-plan areas as it chops a room up into smaller parts, eroding the sense of flow. By layering in rugs and different accents you can still define and zone, distinguishing one area from another – it will just feel more sophisticated if the flooring is continuous.

*Left: Pale floors are great for making a space feel bigger and more open, and lending a comforting visual warmth. They invite you to slow down.*

*Opposite: Concrete floors provide a fabulous neutral base that any style of rug will pair well with, from highly patterned textiles to neutrals. When you contrast the colours with a richly patterned rug, though, you get such a sophisticated vibe.*

The low-down on floors

Not all floors have to match and, although it gives a unified look in bathrooms, kitchens, bedrooms and some other rooms, it's nice to do something a little different so that not everything feels the same. To make this work, go down the co-ordinating route. For example, tie in the colour palette, especially for rooms that are adjacent or where you can see from one room into the next. This will give you cohesiveness and make the transition from room to room appear seamless. One of the best tips I can give you is picking a colour family; this is a tried-and-tested formula I've used for years and it never looks boring.

I tend to avoid (but this is a personal choice) contrasting colours. I might play around with colour values, although again it's all about easing the transition from room to room so it flows and doesn't feel jarring. One more thing is to try not to let more than two floor types meet or touch at any intersection, as that can read as quite messy to the eye.

*Left: Patterned flooring is a fun, creative way to bring personality to rooms – it adds instant pizazz, brightening things up underfoot.*

*Opposite: While matching flooring is an easy way to give your space a unified look, you by no means have to stick to this. When you mix things up, as seen here, it can look unique and intriguing.*

The low-down on floors

# GIVING FLOORS NEW LIFE

Examining all the different flooring options available is essential in helping you make the right decision, not just for your floors but for your whole scheme. If you can, avoid getting caught up in the cycle of what's in and what's out in terms of trends as you will never keep up. Instead, follow your heart – budget permitting.

## RUGS

I am rug-obsessed and have them in every room in the house, as they bring texture, colour, pattern and joy into each of my spaces. You can never have too many rugs in my opinion, from solid hues to metallics, stripes, hand-woven patterns, florals, lavish shagpiles – overdose on them!

Rugs are particularly great if you don't like your current flooring but implementing a permanent and expensive flooring change isn't an option. One of my pet peeves is a bare floor, even in kitchens, and especially in hallways. Don't think that in these more practical spaces you can't have rugs, because you can. Just opt for naturally resistant flat weaves and all sorts of lovely vinyls, as opposed to deep-pile rugs that will trap food and dirt.

Rugs are a great way to give your palette a sounding board, a jumping-off point. I often pick out specific hues from the weave, taking them into my finishing touches, soft furnishings and even furniture. Think of rugs as another foundation to a room; they connect everything through a single grounding point and always set a beautiful tone.

There are no hard-and-fast rules when it comes to choosing colours and patterns. Subconsciously and intuitively, I tend to keep things peaceful and conducive to relaxation in the bedroom, so opt for deep-pile, neutral threads, while in the living room I tend to go a little bolder. I often layer rugs together, or arrange them in groups throughout a space, especially in open-plan spaces. Rugs are great for framing your furniture and generally should be big enough to make an impact.

When it comes to having furniture legs on or off a rug (one of my most frequently asked questions), I would say just be consistent. If your sofa legs are off the rug, have the odd chair off as well, so it looks as intentional as possible. If your rug is a little too small, layer it alongside other rugs and runners.

*Above left: Rugs are a room's 'completers', anchoring everything and bringing things together visually. When you tie them into the palette – wham bam, instant harmony.*

*Above: Going bold or patterned with a rug instantly turns up the volume. Pattern is like a spice, pepping things up and adding so much extra interest.*

You also don't want a rug to swallow up the whole floor, because then it's stepping into carpet territory. In the bedroom, like any room, there are many options. You can frame the whole bed with a large rug, which will anchor the room, or go for a shaggy runner down the side, which will lend warmth and texture. An easy-to-clean flat weave is kid- and food-proof; a round jute rug is lovely under a chair or stool. Irregular shapes give you much more freedom in larger spaces – for example, a cowhide under a coffee table or at the foot of a chair, or a circular rug anchoring a dining table.

In hallways, you want something durable, but I think it's key not to go too plain – pattern immediately establishes your home's personality, and this is just what these often-narrow spaces need. You could pick two tantalizing colours and make a pair, or buddy up kilims with sheepskins. You can also stick to one colour palette and play around with scale for contrast, and any room will always work with rugs crafted from natural fibres like sisal and hemp.

**How to mix multiple rugs in the same room**
The easiest way to make things feel cohesive when it comes to mixing rugs of different patterns and sizes together is to keep them within the same colour family. You can mix anything if they share the same colour palette or family. Having this commonality across multiple rugs will help unify the space so much more.

Additionally, you can mix rugs if they are all quite saturated, or indeed all quite neutral, even if their patterns are different. The trick is to make sure they are all similar weights visually – this makes mixing and matching so easy. You can mix pattern with pattern, pattern with solid, and solid with solid. Solids are a little safer and more conservative, so make them super-textural so they read as visually intriguing. You can also rock the same rug twice – again, this is a safe choice, but it can totally work as long as nothing else in the room matches. One more thing: don't worry if all your rugs are different sizes and shapes. I don't. It creates a relaxed set-up in any room and adds lots of interest.

*Shaggy rugs add instant tactile delight for your feet and are such a luxurious material to walk over, making them perfect for living rooms and bedrooms.*

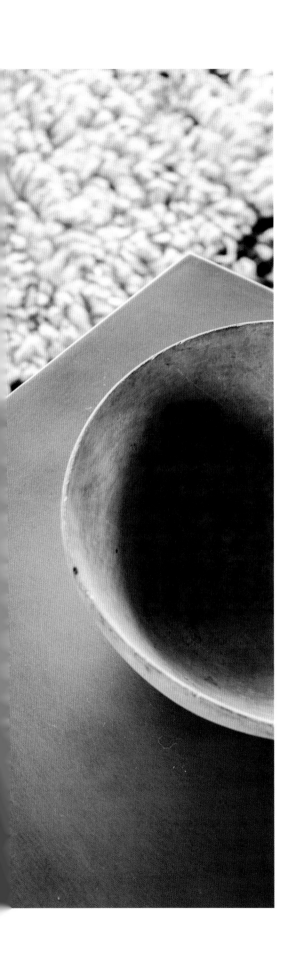

# Six pro tips for selecting rugs

**1.** Large rugs always work as they anchor a room immediately. If you have smaller rugs, make sure you layer in more than one – there is nothing sadder than a single small rug in a room.

**2.** High-traffic areas like hallways and kitchens are better suited to low-pile rugs that are easier to clean than their plusher counterparts. In bedrooms and living rooms, go more shaggy and deep-pile, which feels lovely underfoot.

**3.** Think beyond typical areas and instead layer in rugs on landings, and in hallways, bathrooms and kitchens. If you have blah wall-to-wall carpeting, layering in a colourful dhurrie or vintage Berber rug is a great option.

**4.** Whether it's a small faux sheepskin by the bathtub, a larger Berber rug in the living room, or a jute runner in the hallway, rugs are the easiest way to introduce warmth and texture into a space. Look upon texture as you would a herb or spice when cooking – it adds instant pizazz and elevates everything!

**5.** Patterned or colourful rugs will be far more durable and read as visually more intriguing than solid hues.

**6.** Always add a rug pad as it stops a rug from moving and provides extra cushioning. More importantly, it will prolong the life of the rug by reducing the friction between it and the floor.

# CARPETS

Carpets have had a bit of a bad rap in the past for being boring, beige and quite bland, since these types have dominated the flooring market for years. They're an easy option for landlords and new builds, where they're more or less ubiquitous and an obvious choice for anyone wanting to play it safe. Going for wall-to wall-carpeting is a no-brainer, and it will always work – it's just really hard to decorate around.

However, I happen to think carpets are going through a bit of a transformation, offering up a fresh array of plush coverings in organic fibres, punchy animal prints and wonderfully dense, saturated hues like ochres, pickles and emeralds.

We are now also using them in different ways. It is rarer to see wall-to-wall carpeting in every room of the house. Instead, they are often reserved for bedrooms, dens, TV rooms and playrooms. With comfort, wellbeing and sustainability being at the forefront of many homeowners' priorities, we have more choices than ever before. We can choose from natural fibres like sisal, jute, coir and seagrass (a plant grown in coastal waters that is sustainably sourced and looks beautiful in any room). We can go plush with a velvet-style pile underfoot, or super-relaxed with woollen loops creating a soft and sumptuous environment.

Spending more time at home means having more time to consider options, and there are so many bedazzling patterns, gorgeous textural combinations and incredible colourways to choose from – from geometrics to intricate patterns, and from mismatched colour combos and clashing patterns to earthy, calming and natural hues. Textures and colours that offer comfort and tantalize the senses are very relevant for now.

**Selecting the right carpet**

When choosing a carpet, it is crucial to take into consideration the intended use of the room. There are two major categories of carpet: cut pile and loop pile. In cut-pile carpeting, as the name suggests, the ends of the fibre loops are cut, while in loop-pile carpets they are left looped and uncut. You can get cut-pile plush, which gives a soft, velvety, even finish with a short pile; or cut-pile twist, which is more hardwearing and good for high-traffic areas – it has a textured finish and doesn't show tracking from footprints or vacuuming. Level loop-pile carpets have a distinct, textured look, do not show footprints and are good for areas that see a lot of footfall. Multi-level loop-pile carpets are textural and super-durable and, as the name suggests, provide a textured finish using loops of various heights. Are you confused yet?

*Carpets add warmth to every space, with natural fibres such as wool and cotton being the optimal choice. Opting for richer textures, as here, immediately complements an interior.*

Don't be. In the bedroom you might want a calming and soothing vibe, so opt for a textural neutral in a cut pile, as they are softer underfoot than a loop carpet. In a hallway or study, something more durable would work, like a loop pile. Be clear about the feeling you want to create; patterns and bolder statements, for example, are great for hallways, stairs and landings. These transitional spaces, with their limited amount of space for furniture, can easily take more of a design statement. Plush, textural neutrals are lovely for bedrooms, while animal prints can be great for home offices, adding loads of texture. Stripes are a fabulous way to make a small room appear longer or wider as the optical illusion adds more depth, and if you want to add even more texture, layer an area rug on top of the carpet to make it feel super-luxurious. If you happen to have drab wall-to-wall carpet that you can't replace, then the key to beating the beige is to layer a rug on top. Not only will this break up the flooring by introducing layers of colour and pattern, it will also take the eye away from the carpet beneath. From vintage rugs to contemporary options, this tip will elevate your room no end. Clever, no?

I am rug-obsessed and have them in every room in the house, as they bring texture, colour, pattern and joy into each of my spaces.

# FOCUS ON WOODEN FLOORING

*With their rich tones and beautiful grain, hardwood floors lend warmth and elegance to rooms. Whether you add rugs for a warmer feel or keep an expanse of bare wood, they never go out of fashion.*

*Chevron flooring is both timeless and stylish. Defined by its V shape, it creates distinctive zigzag patterns.*

Hardwood, parquet, engineered, reclaimed boards: selecting the perfect wooden floor is a daunting task. With so much choice out there, never mind whether the boards are sawn plain or flat – both of which affect the finished appearance – it's a minefield. There's no need to panic, though. What follows is everything you need to know about wooden flooring.

*Wide plank flooring makes a room feel bigger and grander. It's the combo of width and length that tricks the eye into believing the room is larger than it really is. Clever, no?*

# Hardwood

Let's start with hardwood floors. Planks are crafted from a single piece of wood and can literally last for ages. If you are starting from scratch, choosing the type of wood and the colour is the fun part. Oak is one of the most durable and widely available woods and it can take stain very well, so can be customized in a variety of finishes, from bleached off-white to ebony. Hickory has lots of colour variation, with both light and dark tones; walnut is richer still; maple and birch are blonder and lighter. If you're unsure which type and colour to go for, consider any other wooden elements you might have in your home. Walnut cabinetry or oak wardrobes could set the tone and, although I say it a lot, if you limit the palette it will make everything feel more tranquil.

How logs are sawn has a big effect on the appearance of the grain and thus the pattern. Flat-sawn boards have a wavy appearance – known as 'cathedral pattern' because their defining feature is arches like those seen in a cathedral; quarter-sawn boards have tiger-style stripes; while rift-sawn boards offer the straightest grain. In general, wider boards look more sophisticated; they are less busy and create the illusion of a larger space. They are also a lot more expensive, so to make your budget go further, you can install wider boards in primary living spaces, and narrow boards in secondary spaces, such as hallways and bedrooms.

There has also been a big increase in bamboo and eucalyptus floors; these can be grown for quick harvesting, making them much more environmentally friendly. Bamboo flooring has a rich, light grain that looks super-stylish. Eucalyptus floors can easily stand up to humidity and moisture, so are great in kitchens, bathrooms and basements. Available in various textures, colours and levels of gloss, both options are also much less expensive than hardwood. Reclaimed wood is another option, salvaged from barns, factories and old buildings. It has a great texture, and its characterful nail holes, cracks and even saw marks are an integral part of the look.

Most hardwood floors are finished with a clear coating of polyurethane to protect them from staining, moisture, and general wear and tear. You can also get oil-based finishes, which feel a bit richer and don't leave a film on top.

# Engineered wood

While hardwood is cut from a log, engineered wood is composed of a thin layer of wood on top of a manufactured base of layered wood such as ply. It won't expand and contract, or warp or shrink as much as real wood. It's also cheaper. Engineered wood can be glued to a slab, whereas hardwood requires a subfloor in order to be nailed in place. It comes in a wide range of wood types, grades and finishes, and lends itself to wide boards – plus it's available in both chevron and parquet patterns, which always look amazing. Engineered wood is the best of both worlds – a top layer of beautiful hardwood and then alternating layers of ply, which make it durable. It is a very feasible option in bathrooms and kitchens, where you have to consider moisture.

*Bringing a natural beauty, hardwood floors are such a versatile option for living rooms. They make a style statement which, when you add softly woven rugs, takes things to another level.*

## TILES

There are many different types of tiles available, from ceramic to porcelain, cement and stone, to name just a few.

Ceramic tiles are probably the most common as they are more affordable than other types; they are also durable, so are perfect in kitchens, bathrooms and entryways. Super-easy to clean, they come in hundreds of styles and finishes, as well as a wide variety of sizes and shapes, from square to rectangular, octagonal to hexagonal. Smaller mosaic tiles are pre-moulded on mesh sheets, so you don't have to set each tile individually, and with tinted grout you can be even more creative.

Porcelain tiles are smooth, quite dense and impermeable, making them suitable for all rooms, including outside. They can emulate natural stone, wood, concrete and even brick. They are a great all-purpose tile and come in a huge array of colours and styles – from bold patterns to softly hued neutrals.

Terracotta tiles are incredibly swoon-worthy. Although many colour variations are available, I am obsessed with the Belgian tiles in darker hues made from unglazed terracotta. These add instant flair and are great in boot rooms, loos or even kitchens.

Brick is one of the most common architectural elements around. Brick flooring is made from thinner bricks than those used for walls, and it has a smoother, less porous surface. Some flooring bricks come in sheets, much like mosaic tiles. These are installed using mortar and can be fitted together in different configurations to create custom patterns. Brick adds visual warmth, colour and texture. Its durability, like any hard floor, has its flip side – it is no more comfortable underfoot than stone or concrete.

Cement tiles, with their seemingly endless design options and impressive durability, have taken the tile world by storm. They shine in the bathroom, adding pops of texture and pattern, while breaking up quite a plain space. They hold up to daily wear and tear, thanks to their unique manufacturing process, and are soft and silky to the touch without being a slip hazard. From neutral and natural shades, to intricate Moorish designs, geometric profiles, bright jewel tones, dark hues and arabesque shapes, they can be customized to create any pattern you can dream of.

Stone tiles are typically installed in kitchens, bathrooms and even hallways, being hardwearing, elegant and sophisticated. They will also never go out of fashion. Your choices are numerous, varying from marble to limestone, granite or travertine, any of which will give you that luxurious look. Polished limestone is uber-contemporary, while travertine is a little more rustic, so it really depends upon your aesthetic. The rich, natural colours, distinct veining and natural characteristics found in stone floors create a timeless treatment that adds a touch of warmth to a space.

The low-down on floors

*Tiles arranged in a herringbone pattern are far more playful and fun than traditional rectangular or square tiles.*

*Cosy brick flooring adds such charm to this bathroom. The mottled hues add warmth and a visual interest often missing in bathrooms.*

## CONCRETE

I am slightly obsessed with concrete floors; they have huge appeal with their visual continuity, compactness and the fact that they look and feel strong and soft at the same time. Undeniably cool, they can be surprisingly inviting and warm and they also combine perfectly well with marble, ceramic, wood – in fact, anything. I also love that there is no grout. You can vary the finish from a subtle glow to a full-blown gloss, and when you layer over rugs, both vintage and modern, you will take these floors to new heights. I generally opt for low sheen as it feels more relaxed and less like a garage floor!

Micro cement is a cement-based coating that can be applied thinly (approx. 2–3mm/⅛in) at a fraction of the cost of concrete. It looks and feels like concrete, yet doesn't require any special laying skills or machinery. It is either mixed by hand or in a mixing vessel, then poured onto a prepared floor and left to dry.

## LAMINATE

For a budget-friendly option, laminate flooring wins hands down. It has come a long way from the bland, fake-looking wood once on offer. From exotic woods to unique finishes, laminate offers realistically distressed surfaces, unusual wood grains and patterns, bevelled edges, and colours that range from milky white to walnut brown. I am particularly obsessed with African, Asian and South American wood finishes – they give you a beautiful floor that looks like it has been made from rare, exotic wood, when it hasn't, and neither has it depleted precious natural resources (or your wallet). Generally, it's one-third to one-half the price of wood or stone, and it takes little time to fit. It can be installed by floating it above an existing surface, unattached to the old floor (obviously this doesn't apply to carpet). Most floors require a polyurethane underlay beneath the planks.

Once taboo (just think of roadside diners and hospital floors), tile-like vinyl laminate has also come a long way. You can now find it with all sorts of super-chic prints, from woodgrain to ceramic, stone and marble. With hundreds of designs, endless configurations and beautiful matt finishes, it has had an extreme fashion makeover. It is also cost-effective and easy to maintain.

The low-down on floors

*Sleek, homely and incredibly durable, concrete floors are undeniably cool. This pared-down material creates an instant feeling of serenity.*

# STYLING YOUR STAIRCASE

You might think it a little odd that I'm singling out the staircase here, but there was a time, not so long ago, when a staircase wasn't seen as purely practical, and instead was a revered focal point – making a statement with its flooring choices, together with super-glam chandeliers and other adornments. Whether you have a few steps, many flights or a winding staircase, I can't stress enough how important it is to make your stairway treads stylish. They are often the first thing you see when you walk through the door and they create an instant first impression.

*Staircases deserve as much decorative attention as any other space in the house. Hanging artwork and employing a beautiful palette turns them into something far more than simply a connecting passageway.*

Look upon your stairs as so much more than just a practical way of getting from A to B, from one floor to another. I honestly feel we need little wow moments throughout our homes – smile-inducing touches as you transition through the space – and what better place is there for this than the stairs, which are so often overlooked. Picking the right flooring is key. Patterns are great for stairs: these high-traffic areas take a lot of wear and tear, and pattern will disguise that. You can choose from fully carpeted stairs, with carpet covering the entire riser, or runners that cover a portion of the stairs, leaving the edges exposed. From leopard print to stripes, bold and daring to neutrals, the possibilities are endless. If you go neutral, add some drama with stair rods.

Painting risers and treads is another option – and contrasting treads can take the effect even further. Whether you go sultry and dark for drama, or airy and neutral, just think about making the stairs grab attention in some way, either texturally or with a bold colour or pattern. With such a small space to cover, you can afford to be a bit more daring in your choices. You can even wallpaper the risers in a cool pattern and use colour in creative ways to draw attention to the floor. I tend to match the risers to the walls so that it feels quite seamless, but this is a very personal thing.

*Painting the treads of your staircase can transform it into something super eye-catching. Not just that, it's a great way to inject colour and detail into a transitional area.*

# STYLE HACKS FOR RENTERS

## Invest in rugs

Layering textiles over existing flooring is a classic move. From runners to rugs, watch how their textures and colours take your floor to a whole new level. Natural-fibre rugs also create a lovely foundation, concealing and elevating your floor at the same time.

## Lay temporary tiles

Peel-and-stick tiles allow you to (sneakily) cover up an undesirable floor with little effort!

## Add low seating

Conceal the floor with a few well-placed pouffes or floor cushions – they are excellent distractors.

## Roll your own flooring

Vinyl rolls or sheets with realistic textures make good temporary flooring options as they can be rolled out (as long as the subfloor is clean and flat). For extra security, use double-sided tape to prevent movement.

*Moving into a rented home can mean dealing with design elements you wouldn't have chosen yourself. The best way to distract from them is with a beautiful bold rug.*

No landlord permission required here, check out how to distract the eye and make your space feel more high-end, regardless of the flooring that's in place when you move in.

*Opting for rugs that complement existing flooring always makes a space feel sophisticated and subtle.*

# Top 5 flooring trends: boards and beyond

**1.** If you've inherited wooden floors but they've seen better days, like I did in my house, rather than ripping them out, consider painting or staining them. It's so much more cost-effective than completely replacing them, and the look is timeless. There's been a move away from white and airy towards darker, more saturated hues recently, but this is a very personal choice. I would say that with darker floors it's easier to see any imperfections, but I love them.

**2.** Hexagonal tiles, particularly the smaller ones, are having a moment. They are great in bathrooms, shower areas or niches, and come in many different colours and textures. They're a fab option for high-traffic areas.

**3.** If you are replacing your flooring, wide boards always look more expensive than narrow ones. They look grander, more luxurious and they are so very beautiful.

**4.** Herringbone and chevron patterns shout elegant Parisian apartment. Classic and timeless, they've been around forever and will always work. Both patterns have wonderful movement, creating an elegant sophistication.

**5.** Grey-toned floors are the go-to neutral, just as beige once was. Offering greater depth, they work with any scheme and style and they will never date.

When it comes to choosing the flooring treatment that is right for you, don't get caught up with what is in right now. If you love a trend, by all means embrace it, but ultimately you should go for flooring that makes you happy, has longevity and will provide the perfect base you can add to, all while creating a scheme that will remain timeless!

# GARY MARSHALL AND KEITH HIRST
## Textural drama

There's an incredible beauty in the dialogue between the rough brick walls, bare plastered surfaces and exposed copper piping, along with other industrial hard finishes.

The low-down on floors

*A beautiful sculptural staircase runs the entirety of the house and, against a backdrop of soft, warm brick, lends the space a cosy, sophisticated and calming vibe.*

Located in the conservation area of Ramsgate, on the south-east English coast, Gary Marshall and Keith Hirst's seaside house has been completely redesigned as a dramatic, warehouse-style home, with a focus on materiality and scale. This incredible renovation is set over four floors, and involved removing a side section of the building to create a full-height void that uses external and internal light to add volume.

With a private courtyard set behind Crittall-style doors, a roof terrace, three bedrooms and an open-plan kitchen, dining and living area, it is a stunning home that embraces materiality. The kitchen has been fitted with bespoke steel cabinetry, micro-cement worktops and timber flooring, while exposed brick and bare plaster walls add textural interest throughout. A cantilevered staircase runs up the entire left side of the building, letting light in through its perforated sides, and it echoes the metalwork in the kitchen superbly.

*Right: The lines between outdoors and indoors are beautifully blurred, with the green palette carrying through into the kitchen cabinetry.*

*Far right: Rooms were sacrificed for higher ceilings, which lend real grandeur to the villa.*

The low-down on floors

The low-down on floors

There's an incredible beauty in the dialogue between the rough brick walls, bare plastered surfaces and exposed copper piping, along with other industrial hard finishes like the metalwork of the staircase. Everything has some kind of texture, including the mix of traditional and contemporary furnishings and accessories. It is a home that feels dramatic, exciting and yet also relaxing, as flashes of luxe materials in the living areas and bedrooms offset the industrial hardness. It's a lovely combination in my book, and a truly memorable home that feels curated, individual and compelling, all at the same time.

*Below: The combination of plaster and brick walls tells such an artful story. Employing historical references, Gary and Keith have crafted a home that feels original, deeply relevant and incredibly personal.*

*Opposite: Decades of time-worn plaster give the bedroom walls the most beautiful patina.*

*Overleaf: The ground-floor space is imbued with intimacy and texture, while the integrity of the architecture shines through. It's chic, unpretentious and seriously alluring.*

The low-down on floors

# ACCESSORIES AND ACCENTS

No matter how much time and energy you've put into designing a room – choosing the most perfect pieces of furniture, the right lights, an amazing palette – sometimes it still feels as if there's something missing. Maybe it's just a little too bland or too perfectly polished. You feel blocked, so what can you do?

More often than not it comes down to accessories – otherwise known as finishing touches, or what I like to call the five-minute face-lifters of the decorating world. Accessories lift everything, and by adding them into your scheme they will reconnect you to what you love – memories, journeys, stories – and shift the perspective of your home. While there aren't any hard-and-fast rules when it comes to accessorizing, there are lots of tricks. Knowing which style or styles you gravitate towards is the first thing to address.

Are you a mid-century minimalist or a boho maximalist? Even if you can't quite figure out exactly which style you're drawn to, don't worry – simply mix together styles that you love, rather than replicating a specific look. In general, most people stick to around three core styles, but it's absolutely fine to mix more into the equation. I've seen up to ten different styles in a room working wonderfully well together – just remember to restrict the number of colours, repeat materiality and then mix away.

Accessories can give you just as much bang for your buck as spectacular chandeliers and gallery-esque art. These eye-catching details and accents grab your attention and elevate surfaces and walls to the highest degree. From mirrors to art, candles, books, sculptures, planters, flowers, curtains, clocks, trays, stools, pouffes and figurines, visual inspiration comes in so many different forms.

Accessories take homes to a whole new level, and although they may seem unimportant by themselves, when layered together they contribute so much to the atmosphere and cosiness of a room. Learning how to style these pieces will make your home feel more beautiful and covetable. This chapter provides your essential tool kit – never again will you look at your home and ask yourself why it doesn't work!

*When styling any shelf, mantelpiece or console, create a layered look that lets each piece shine. Make sure everything isn't the same height, which can make displays feel too clunky and heavy. And rather than leaving gaps, overlap – the effect will be far more intriguing.*

Accessories and accents

# Success with accessories

1. Shop your wardrobe. Check out your own favourite colours and styles!

2. Identify your signature colour (and use it everywhere).

3. Add in highlights and lowlights.

4. Use a combo of cool and warm colour tones.

5. Practise the art of layering.

6. Embrace the rule of three.

7. Stay away from too much tone-on-tone and mix up your materials.

*Above left: Shelves are taken to another level by weaving in accessories. As practical as this shoe cupboard may be, with the accessories beautifully curated there is no need for doors.*

*Above: Balance is created through groups. A little cluster of objects of varying heights in a combination of materials, textures and finishes elevates a tablescape.*

Accessories and accents

Accessories and accents

# Success with accessories in detail

**1.** Shopping your wardrobe is a fabulous way to see at a glance what you gravitate towards, colour-wise and style-wise. Our clothes tell us a great deal and are a wonderful starting point. For instance, if you have mainly caramels, creams and lots of neutrals in your closet, go for a similar colour palette with your accessories. If you have lots of print, embrace this in the finishing touches by adding in hand-dyed linens, patterned dhurries and pouffes, intricate vases, tea-lights and picture frames. Are your clothes more casual than formal; preppy or pretty? If your style is formal, include tapered accessories, metallic accents, warm wood finishes, statement mirrors and luxe fabrics. If your vibe is a little more relaxed and casual, throw in washed linens, soft woods and aged patinas. From bold designs and lots of colour, to neutrals and textures, mirroring that aesthetic ensures that you will always come home to a house that makes you happy.

**2.** Have a jumping-off colour that you use time and time again – for me it's black. I constantly incorporate a deep, inky hue in art, tea-lights, black tapered candles and vases. I use it everywhere.

**3.** Introduce highlights and lowlights and mix them together: highlights are brighter and lowlights are softer and more subtle. Lighter and darker shades work beautifully together, so when combining accessories, use both.

**4.** Mix up cool tones and warm tones, as all rooms need a variety. Let's take my lower-ground floor as an example. I have lots of warm pinks, oranges, reds, browns and beiges – combined with greens, greys and whiter, cooler tones – and they look amazing together.

**5.** Embrace the art of layering. This adds depth as it involves placing items either in front of or behind something. When you layer up different design elements, the whole room automatically feels textured and unique. You can also easily enhance the sense of cosiness by overlapping, leaning pieces in, or stacking them on top of one another.

**6.** According to the rule of three, things arranged in odd numbers are more pleasing – your eye is forced to move further around the grouping, which makes for a more interesting visual experience.

**7.** Make sure you don't just pick out tone-on-tone colours. Although they are always beautiful, at times they can feel a little flat. If you love the tone-on-tone look (and I certainly do), make sure you really mix up the materiality between pieces to keep things looking interesting.

*Anything tumbling and trailing over shelves or tables is a must, immediately softening the vignette and drawing the eye.*

# TIPS FOR ARRANGING ACCESSORIES

Decorating becomes much simpler, more joyful and less stressful when you know the styling tricks that designers use. A huge amount of what I do, aside from identifying how a room functions and flows, is concerned with how a room feels. The ambience of a space is so important. This is where the obsessive in me comes into play. I love nothing more than creating self-contained worlds through my accessories – beautiful moments and stories that show our friends and family what our interests are and what makes us happy. Creating vignettes around collections of things you love results in personalized, welcoming interiors that anyone entering the house will instantly pick up on.

When it comes to creating several arrangements in a room, make sure they harmonize and balance with one another so that they look intentional. One vignette shouldn't appear more heavily styled than another, or have more pattern or colour; they should all relate. Having said that, and to confuse you a little further, creating contrast – or friction, as I like to call it – in your accessories and the way they are styled is of paramount importance. Friction correlates directly to interest or energy. If there is no friction, or very little, rooms feel flat; if there is too much contrast, spaces can feel chaotic. I advise being somewhere in the middle. You can create contrast through texture, pattern, shape, size, colour and style. Bear in mind that opposites attract. Opposing textures, such as flat weaves with slubby shaggy weaves, work beautifully together. Opposing styles – for example, modern with vintage – also look better than, say, Scandi and mid-century modern, which are both about natural shapes, minimal silhouettes and calming palettes; those styles are a little too similar, so nothing really stands out. It's far more intriguing to mix up decorative styles – that way, interiors always look more compelling.

I tend to go for maybe three or four styles, but six or seven different looks can also work. Just make sure you use a restricted palette – too many different styles and colours will read like a hot mess!

*This arrangement is such a good example of the way that a restricted palette makes accessories look curated and considered.*

From mirrors to
art, candles, books,
sculptures, planters,
flowers, curtains, clocks,
trays, stools, pouffes
and figurines, visual
inspiration comes in so
many different forms.

# FAIL-SAFE FORMULAS FOR SURFACES

When styling surfaces, whether that be mantels, shelves, coffee tables or consoles, always think about creating depth and adding variety. Tablescaping is the art of transforming a surface into something magical. By adding a few bits and bobs, you can create the most engaging narrative, turning a surface into a beautifully curated vignette.

There is some skill involved here. You can't, for instance, create an effective tablescape by placing three similar-sized vases on a console – this would read as quite bland. Our eyes are bored by repetition, so constantly think about adding something horizontal, something vertical and then something a little more sculptural. Always play around with heights, too. For consoles banking walls, and any shelves or mantels, adding something vertical (especially if it's large) is a game-changer. This could be a big mirror, a piece of art, a tall vase holding a collection of branches – anything that draws the eye upwards. For something horizontal, a stack of books, or a collection of beautiful storage boxes, should be permanently on your radar. Make sure to add another object on top, to break up all those straight lines. This could be something a little more curvaceous and organic, such as a lovely bowl of roses or a sweet sculpture.

When it comes to placing accessories, never put them in rows (practically a criminal offence). Instead, arrange pieces in front of each other to create depth, with the third accessory off to one side, or on top of a stack of books or storage boxes. If you have a large lamp at the end of a console, rather than repeating it at the other end, go for something with similar visual weight, like a pot, so that it feels balanced. Take the eye up, along and down, continually creating points of interest – much like a city skyline.

*Always start with the tallest piece at the back or to one side, then layer in any small or medium pieces accordingly.*

# MORE ON MY FAVOURITES

While we all have different tastes and different definitions of what makes the perfect accessory, my arsenal always includes lamps, artwork, plants, soft furnishings, books, ornaments, candles, bowls, trays and mirrors. These pieces add instant ambience and I've never known a wall or surface that wasn't transformed by them. They take things to another level and really make a space come alive.

## MY GO-TO ACCESSORIES

Lamps
Art
Botanicals
Cushions, rugs and throws
Books
Vases, pots and sculpture
Tea-lights and candles
Bowls
Trays
Mirrors

*Left: Repetition – of colours, materials or textures – is a great styling trick, helping to pull a scheme together.*

*Opposite: Creative styling is all about elevating surfaces with pieces that tell a story. The most beautifully designed schemes take your eye on a journey around the whole room, with so many varied heights, compelling textures and different finishes that you don't quite know where to look.*

## LAMPS

Overdose on lamps: put them everywhere and anywhere. Add a lamp to any tabletop, or place a light in any corner that's a little dull. They create the softest, most wonderful glow and make staying at home the only thing you'll want to do. You can create drama by going supersized, or pull surfaces together with a collection of sweet little lamps. They add warmth, character and so much dimension. The right lighting also stimulates our senses. Ceiling lighting should be on a dimmer so you can control the mood and create a tranquil atmosphere when needed, and as disussed in Chapter 2, all lighting should be layered, with a mix of ambient, accent and task lighting creating the most beautiful vibe.

I am super-obsessed with cordless lamps, which are flexible, portable and perfect for indoor and outdoor spaces; they are so versatile I have them everywhere.

## ART

Art is another great way to add personality to surfaces; it will always make things look lovely and more meaningful. Whether you're looking for a quick refresh or starting from scratch, art is something you can constantly add to, helping you build a warm, relaxing haven and enlivening your walls, all at the same time.

## BOTANICALS

Say goodbye to drab surfaces forever by using botanicals. Whether that's a bunch of dried berries and seedpods – their unexpected texture primed to steal the limelight on tablescapes – or something gathered or foraged from the garden or hedgerows, botanicals always upscale a tabletop. I constantly have little glasses of bay and rosemary on rotation in the kitchen, or lichen-laden branches acting as the centrepiece on my dining table, or even bundles of trailing eucalyptus tumbling over my kitchen shelves. There is such a quiet charm in bringing the outside in – it sets a restful mood, transforming a coffee table, shelf or table in need of attention. I'm also deeply influenced by the seasons and the landscape, and like nothing better than tracing the arc of the seasons with my botanicals. This means my surfaces never stay the same; they are always evolving, with items that mirror the season, providing movement and wonderful silhouettes.

*Left: No tablescape is ever complete without plants to add life, colour and texture.*

*Opposite: I change my botanicals according to the seasons, so grasses and meadow flowers for the warmer months, and branches and drooping fronds for the cooler months. These textural puffs of grass will gently sway with the breeze, bringing a quiet charm to this windowsill.*

## CUSHIONS, RUGS AND THROWS

When it comes to soft furnishings, draping throws over chairs, sofas and beds, plopping cushions on sofas and chairs, and placing pouffes and skimming rugs on floors always ups the cosy factor. These give our rooms so much more character and texture, and they always feel inviting. Although they are considered purely decorative, never underestimate the power they have to pull a room together, revamping a dull space, or giving a room a seasonal refresh. They are the interiors equivalent of a cheeky pre-dinner cocktail – an instant pick-me-up!

## BOOKS

Stocking up on books gives you the perfect tool for adding an extra dimensional flourish to coffee tables, consoles and shelves. I'm always stacking books on their sides on nightstands and tables, and then topping them with candles, plants, flowers or something super-sculptural. They are fabulous for coffee tables, long shelves and consoles, adding an immediate structural dimension, and they instantly make a home feel curated and more lived in.

## VASES, POTS AND SCULPTURE

I am a little vase-obsessed, and love to have examples that are at the crossroads of modernity and tradition on all my surfaces. I like to collect pieces with a rare spirit and sensibility – those that almost impart traces of the hands that crafted them – and I happen to believe that surfaces should never be empty, but instead covered with characterful items that you cherish.

Don't forget to add something a little off-radar – something random to pique the interest; this will automatically make your room feel more intriguing. Dotted throughout my house I have quite a few old stone busts and some cool art that I've picked up from flea markets, along with an unusual sculpture propped by the fire and a funny little stool I found in France. What you don't want is the feeling that your home has been plucked out of a catalogue, with everything feeling and looking precious, sterile and just so.

*Cushions, throws and pouffes are the finishing touches of the decorating world – a little 'five-minute facelift', if you like – transforming rooms with their soft appeal.*

## TEA-LIGHTS AND CANDLES

Tea-lights and candles add a lovely warmth to surfaces by diffusing light in the most beautiful way, so if you add just one element to set the mood it should be these. Good lighting in the form of sparkly tea-lights and candles is a game-changer at any time of year.

## TRAYS

Trays introduce a unique form, function and materiality to surfaces. This styling trick works in the bathroom, kitchen, living room and dining room, so trays are an accessory I use time and time again. From delicate and classic, like rattan or glass, to unique and lovely, like leather-bound or marble, in my book every surface needs a tray. Large, small, contemporary, artisan, they cosy up surfaces instantly, and corral separate items beautifully. Relatively inexpensive and super-versatile, trays help you reduce clutter as your brain will interpret whatever is on them as one element as opposed to lots of separate pieces – they really do turn a bunch of random things into a single, unified collection. Botanicals work wonderfully, from foliage plants to flowers and single stems, as do candles, books, glasses and, of course, tea-lights. Kitcheny things also look good – I have my salt and pepper pots, little bowl of lemons and a jug of spoons all on a tray. And in the bathroom, a tray holds soaps, flannels and toothbrushes.

## MIRRORS

Every room should have a mirror – they are a designer's secret weapon and one of the most important accessories out there. In fact, I think every room should have more than one mirror. They add depth, bounce the light around, expand horizons, trick the eye, add style – I could go on. Mirrors make spaces feel sophisticated and often, if you go supersized, they are all you need on a wall. Gallery wall stress over! Every mirror that has gone up in my house (and as I write, I have three in my studio alone) has always made the room look better. For example, I have a convex mirror in my studio and a extra-large round mirror, as well as rectangular mirrors in my living room, plus a little raffia mirror over my daybed. In the hallway I've supersized again, and then on one wall I have five little mirrors all hanging together. Mirrors look good everywhere and I never, ever tire of them. Propped against the floor, hung on the wall, casually leaning on a mantel, they are the one accessory that always enhances a room. Obviously, they add a decorative touch, but beyond that they make rooms feel larger and brighter – they have magical powers. They balance rooms out, make a statement, work as an accent, add an inviting touch, connect and link spaces, and create interest all at the same time. I told you I was obsessed!

*Every room needs a mirror: they expand horizons, add depth and create intrigue. Just make sure something cool is reflected back in the glass and – if you can – supersize them. They add such grandeur to a space.*

Accessories and accents 217

# HOW TO NAIL GROUPINGS

There are also other things to consider when it comes to accessorizing. For example, are your consoles and tables round, oval or rectangular? If they are round, create groupings in a triangular shape to make the table visually more interesting. Start with a focal point – this is where my vases and botanicals come in – and then break up the surface by layering in other objects, such as a stack of books with a candle on top or a sculpture. For rectangular or square tables, overdose on trays to house things like remotes or candles together. Add in different levels of books, from large to small. You can also break them up with flowers, stacked boxes and candles. Add in the odd additional decorative object, then finish off with tea-lights and lamps. Nailed!

*Right: Groups of three always work, as odd numbers are more pleasing to the eye. If you don't get the grouping right straight away, just re-address it. I call this 'pottering' – it's one of my favourite pastimes.*

*Opposite: The groupings of items on the two tables here are subdued and subtle, so they don't detract from the statement botanical display.*

# Whipping up a centrepiece

**1.** Choose a statement object for your table. This could be a figurine, a beautiful pot or a lovely piece of decorative glass.

**2.** If you want more, consider a collection of things, such as a grouping of vases or tea-lights. Remember always to vary the heights, as that reads as far more intriguing.

**3.** When it comes to botanicals, branches and foliage are guaranteed to add texture and quite often height, which is super-important for visual interest. Potted plants like ferns and succulents also look great on a main table.

**4.** Often I will chose one central arrangement and then place smaller groupings of tea-lights beneath it. This is simple and easy to do but works so well.

**5.** Lighting is really important, particularly during the festive season: from battery-operated fairy lights to votives, a flickering, flattering glow creates the most wonderful mood.

**6.** Add in metallic accents like candle holders and trays; their shiny surfaces will bounce the light around the room beautifully.

**7.** Think about pulling your tablescape out to the edges – not everything should be centred.

**8.** When shopping, be open to inspiration. Anything handmade always looks stunning, such as bowls crafted from papier-mâché, while vintage pieces such as serving platters or glassware add a unique touch.

**9.** Break out the candles. Being super-slender, no sight lines are blocked, and they add immediate elegance. Candles always make everyone look gorgeous, too. Traditionalists might insist that tapers should only be white, but I disagree. I think you can be more rebellious and spice up any table with something a little more exciting, like earthy colours or deep, inky darks.

*My go-to decorating trick for tables is a vase housing some large branches. It's the simplest thing to do and a great way of bringing the outdoors in. Sculptural, wild, seasonal and natural – and let's not forget the verticality they offer, drawing the eye up!*

# ELEVATING SHELVES

It's quite a big ask to make shelving in your home look interesting, curated and stylish, rather than a dumping ground for random treasures, old magazines and who knows what else. One of the most transformative things I did to my shelves was to stack books both vertically and horizontally. After performing this simple trick, I felt my shelves could actually breathe. I know this may sound over the top, but if you pepper the colours of your books throughout the shelf or bookcase so that not all the lighter books are up at one end and the brighter colours down the other, it will feel far more balanced. I also like to add objects to my horizontal stacks of books to break up the row of spines and elevate the look of the whole bookcase. It's important to mix in vases, plants, lighting and objects of varying heights and styles – just remember to restrict the colour palette so it all feels considered.

Adding art to bookcases always works, too, as it draws the eye to something other than just books, and it takes up more visual real estate. I also hang art off the façade of the bookcase. Hanging framed portraits, prints and ephemera from the partitions of shelves is a creative, artistic approach to take. It takes layering to new heights and imparts a cabinet-of-curiosities-type vibe.

*When it comes to styling shelves, adding in height is key. Too many small things look cluttered and our overall goal is to make the shelving unit feel curated and considered. Restrict the palette (always) and repeat, repeat repeat: materiality, textures, finishes and colours.*

# CREATING A
# HOTEL-WORTHY
# SCENE

You know that feeling you get when you check into a cool hotel, lakeside inn, country retreat or beautiful spa? Excited but also instantly restored; exhilarated but chilled. And you've only just walked through the door! I'm not just talking about crisp, freshly laundered sheets or towels, although there is definitely something in that. Instead, I'm talking soothing palettes, lovely scents and phenomenal detailing. From softly glowing, atmospheric lamps to bohemian-inspired plastered walls, artisanal woven accessories and timeless raw, tactile wooden furniture, all our senses are tantalized.

Aroma is the go-to accessory used by all resorts to evoke feelings of serenity, or indeed energy – it instantly transports you to another place. From candles to essential oils, with scents like ocean mist and sea salt, to deeply resinous amber incense, fragrance immediately elevates our mood. Scent is so often neglected, as most people think in visual terms, and yet it is a key component in creating a complete experience. I am super-obsessed with it. For example, in my hallway I like to create an instant sensory impression, so my fragrances have base notes of oud, oak and cedar – subtle, calming and, most importantly, welcoming. In the living room I'm drawn to spicier notes like cardamom, wood smoke, mimosa and tobacco. In the bedroom I like something more resinous and calming, such as frankincense. And in the kitchen I favour sandalwood, patchouli, eucalyptus and clove. Adding evocative scents acts as a final finishing touch, giving the room an extra dimension.

Luxurious textiles like sheepskins and faux fur cushions, throws crafted from the softest merino wools or velvets, softly woven rugs and linen bedding, upscale rooms immediately. One of the greatest tricks when it comes to accessorizing your space is to remember to create depth so that the eye moves around the room and doesn't get bored. This means that all areas need to be layered up – not necessary crammed with stuff, but you can create lots of quiet little bases that pull a room together.

Remember to add in a few unexpected pops of colour to keep things interesting. A vase of deep red roses, perhaps a burnt-orange cushion – pieces that will act as an instant focal point or highlight to draw the eye. Remember to add pattern-rich pieces into rooms, too, as this enlivens them like nothing else. I realize that introducing pattern can seem a little intimidating, but in my book, rooms without it are a little lacking in personality. You can go super-low-risk with pattern – I'm talking a few cushions or the odd vase or throw – and it will still add so much more dimension.

Another way to introduce pattern is through art. I do this a lot and it breaks up all the solid hues in my rooms really well. Large-patterned sofas, chairs or bed linen may feel a little bold, but if you go for subtler colours, they can be transformative. I always make sure my rugs are patterned as they can add a great deal to a room, packing a punch in subtle – or sometimes colourful – ways. Since not everything is patterned, the effect is lively but not overwhelming. I would never be quite brave enough to pair a boldly patterned sofa with a patterned rug and patterned cushions, as this would be a little too energizing for me, but I do see the power in taking things to the next level when pattern comes into play. This can be through soft furnishings like curtains, rugs and cushions, and even through art, ceramics and trays. I am obsessed with mixing patterns in similar colour families as it tones everything down and looks super-gorgeous. Don't worry about staying within scale or keeping styles similar – just create harmony by adhering to your palette. I often bring texture to the pattern game, too, as it's a way of weaving in a delicate, barely there pattern while also contributing to a harmonious feel.

*There are plenty of ways to make rooms worthy of a swoon-worthy five-star hotel. Start with an intoxicating palette, think about adding atmospheric lighting and make sure your finishes are super-luxe.*

# Some final tips and tricks

**1.** If your room doesn't feel finished, always add black. Black adds dimension and it's a trick designers use all the time for impact. You don't need a lot, but using black will ground and tie a room together, so when it comes to accessories, put black on repeat.

**2.** Place mirrors on top of consoles and cabinets – this will always create the illusion of more depth and make the whole area sparkle.

**3.** Layer, layer and layer again; your accessories will work together to create intrigue and depth.

**4.** Add something a little imperfect: a threadbare rug, a wonky shade, bookshelves brimming with well-thumbed books, casually arranged. The vibe will instantly feel looser, more lived-in and, in my opinion, more beautiful.

**5.** If you vary the sizes of the pillows on beds and sofas it will make rooms feel so much more high-end. A no-fail cushion combo is 60 × 60cm (24 × 24in), 50 × 50cm (20 × 20in) and 40 × 40cm (16 × 16in).

**6.** For foolproof flower arrangements, always group the same flowers together, loosely arranged, and always have the heads just toppling over the vase so that you never see the stems – unless of course it's a branch, and then it's all about the stem!

**7.** Repetition is key with accessories, fabrics, colour and materiality; it ups the luxury level and makes a space feel much more sophisticated.

**8.** If you have a painting that looks too small on a wall, offset it; that way it will feel more curated and the negative space will become part of the image.

Without accessories a room will always feel unfinished and sterile. The paint colour might be perfect, but without mirrors or artwork the walls will feel empty. That sofa side table might be the loveliest and most functional out there, but without books and a gorgeous lamp, it will lack personality. By adding beautiful, personal touches, you are completing the décor while also telling your own story and making your space unique.

*Even in a busy kitchen, a black wall adds a sense of tranquillity and creates a sober contrast with the tableware.*

Accessories and accents

# MILANESE MAGIC
Music and art take centre stage in this moody apartment

Reminiscent of the old jazz clubs you might happen upon
in Paris, the dark, saturated colours feel almost velvety and
are very theatrical.

Accessories and accents

*Nailing the right shade of red isn't easy but when you do land on the right one it injects a space with instant energy and style. Its rich warmth has beautiful undertones that enhance both furnishings and accessories.*

Accessories and accents

This former home of a jazz singer is fantastically atmospheric. Located in a small historic square in the centre of the Italian city of Milan, the incredible apartment, with its warm, relaxing hues, immediately makes you want to shut yourself away and spend time in each and every area. You feel like you have crossed into a magical world full of books, objects, photographs and records. Your eye doesn't quite know where to land, and that makes everything feel so intriguing. You are pulled in many different directions, yet the design remains utterly cohesive.

This is a home that connects with and reflects eclectic passions, with a mix of vintage pieces; from 17th-century Asian artefacts to Eames chairs, everything is combined with such skill. It is an impactful space, which effortlessly combines periods, styles, places and travels in one incredible melting pot.

The colour palette takes things to a whole new level of coolness: the reds, greys and blacks feel soulful and grounding. Reminiscent of the old jazz clubs you might happen upon in Paris, the dark, saturated colours feel almost velvety and are very theatrical. From the living room to the bedroom, bathroom and kitchen, everything feels inviting. The dark walls manage to expand the space, too, by adding depth – especially in smaller rooms like the kitchen and bathroom.

*Opposite: The dining room has a magical ability to draw you in. From the beautiful chandelier to the curtains and books, the eye is drawn across the room in a balanced and controlled fashion. Every vista is beautiful.*

*Below: White makes a chic statement in the apartment, from the supersized windows to the furniture, soft furnishings and accessories. When you put a colour on repeat it always creates a sense of sophistication.*

Accessories and accents

The scene-stealing darks are complemented by some lofty whites and paler tones, such as the cabinetry in the kitchen, the lighter sofa and some artwork, and these lovely accents offset the richer, darker colours beautifully.

What is particularly clever is the use of red – an inherently bold colour. This takes centre stage on the walls and internal doors of the hallway to the bedroom, and appears in various furnishings throughout. But rather than feeling overpowering, the depth of the colour creates a very sophisticated elegance.

When you step into this apartment, the wonderful art, the incredible collection of jazz records and all the fabulous accessories instantly lift your mood. It's such a personal space – once over the threshold, a guest would never want to leave this glamorous, eclectic and most beautiful of homes.

These pages: Surrounding yourself with pieces that you love ensures instant character. This happy personal collection makes the apartment feel complete.

Overleaf: From the supersized artwork to the intoxicating colour palette, the living room has the appeal of haute couture. The pieces have been bound together with such flair, creating a look that is flamboyant and dramatic, with a nod to tradition – it's timeless, classic and beautiful!

# INDEX

# PICTURE CREDITS

Every effort has been made to contact copyright holders of images used in this book. The publisher would be pleased to rectify any omissions in future printings.

Front & back cover: Charles Urmston; p2–6: Charles Urmston; p8: Photo: Monica Spezia/Living Inside; p9: @ living4media/Brandajs, Laurent; p10: Lisa Cohen/Taverne Agency; p11: @ FLC/ADAGP, Paris and DACS, London 2022./@ ADAGP, Paris and DACS, London 2022, Photo: Nathalie Krag/Living Inside, Styling: Roberta Brambilla, Interior Designer: Studio 2046; p12–13: Charles Urmston; p15: Tessa Jol/Taverne Agency; p17: Graham Atkins-Hughes; p18: Charles Urmston; p19: Lisa Cohen/Taverne Agency; p20l: Anna Malmberg/Taverne Agency, Stylist: Mari Strenghielm; p20–21: Charles Urmston; p21r: Taran Wilkhu; p22–23: Anna Malmberg/Taverne Agency, Stylist: Mari Strenghielm; p24: Photo: Johan Sellén/Living Inside, Stylist: Gill Renlund, Owners: Buster & Punch founders; p27: Mikkel Vang/Taverne Agency; p29l: Mark Anthony Fox; p29r: Photo: Nathalie Krag/Living Inside, Styling: Roberta Brambilla, Interior Designer: Studio 2046; p30l: Photo: Johan Sellén/Living Inside, Stylist: Gill Renlund, Owners: Buster & Punch founders; p30r: Photo: Monica Spezia/Living Inside; p31–32: Graham Atkins-Hughes; p35l: Photo: Monica Spezia/Living Inside; p35r: Photo: Monica Spezia/Living Inside, Styling: Fulvia Carmagnini, Owner: Sophie Wannenes – founder of Narkisso; p36: Charles Urmston; p37: Mark Anthony Fox; p39: Michael Sinclair/Taverne Agency, Styling: Laura Fulmine; p40–41: Lina Ostling/Taverne Agency, Stylist: Mari Strenghielm; p42–43: Mikkel Vang/Taverne Agency; p46: @ living4media/von Einsiedel, Andreas; p48: Anna Malmberg/Taverne Agency; p49: @ living4media/Are Media; p50–51: Prue Ruscoe/Taverne Agency; p53: Michael Sinclair/Taverne Agency, Styling: Laura Fulmine; p54–61: Photography: Nicole Franzen; p63: Michael Sinclair/Taverne Agency, Styling: Laura Fulmine; p65: Photo: Johan Sellén/Living Inside, Stylist: Gill Renlund, Owners: Buster & Punch founders; p66l: Mark Anthony Fox; p66r: Anna Malmberg/Taverne Agency, Stylist: Mari Strenghielm; p67: John Carey/Rosendale Design; p68–70: Photo: Monica Spezia/Living Inside; p73l: Anna Malmberg/Taverne Agency, Stylist: Mari Strenghielm; p73r: Mikkel Vang/Taverne Agency; p74: Mark Anthony Fox; p75: @ living4media/Are Media; p77: John Carey/Rosendale Design; p79l: Charles Urmston; p79r: Photo: Krista Keltanen/Living Inside, Styling: Mirsa Kaartinen, Owners: Kati and Tobias Tommila; p81: John Carey/Rosendale Design; p82–85: Charles Urmston; p87: @ living4media/Hej.Hem Interior; p88: Mikkel Vang/Taverne Agency; p91: Dana van Leeuwen/Taverne Agency; p92–93: Tessa Jol/Taverne Agency; p95: @ living4media/Hej.Hem Interior; p96: Photo: Regild Christoffer/Living Inside, Styling: Maja Regild, Owners: &Schufl; p97–99l: Anna Malmberg/Taverne Agency, Stylist: Mari Strenghielm; 99r: Photography: Yassen Hristov/Alicja T./Photofoyer, Stylist: Patrycja Rabinska, designed by InsideArch; p100l: Photo: Nathalie Krag/Living Inside, Styling and produced by Tami Christiansen, Owner: Kristian Lillelund owner of RUM4 interior design; p100r: Photo: Regild Christoffer/Living Inside, Styling: Maja Regild, Owners: &Schufl; p103–109: John Carey/Rosendale Design; p111: Anna Malmberg/Taverne Agency, Stylist: Mari Strenghielm; p113: Photo: Nathalie Krag/Living Inside, Owner: Niles Strøyer Christophersen the young founder and creative director of Danish design brand Frama; p114–115: Charles Urmston; p116: Anna Malmberg/Taverne Agency, Stylist: Mari Strenghielm; p117: Photo: Michael Paul/Living Inside, Owner: Joris Van Apers; p118: Photo: Regild Christoffer/Living Inside, Styling: Maja Regild, Owners: &Schufl; p119: Graham Atkins-Hughes; p120: Photo: Nathalie Krag/Living Inside, Owner: Niles Strøyer Christophersen the young founder and creative director of Danish design brand Frama; p121: Michael Sinclair/Taverne Agency, Styling: Laura Fulmine; p123: Mark Anthony Fox; p124–125: Charles Urmston; p126: Lina Ostling/Taverne Agency, Stylist: Mari Strenghielm; p127: Charles Urmston; p128: Photo: Nathalie Krag/Living Inside, Styling and produced by Tami Christiansen, Owner: Kristian Lillelund owner of RUM4 interior design; p129: Photo: Monica Spezia/Living Inside; p131l: Photo: Krista Keltanen/Living Inside, Styling: Jonna Kivilahti; p131r: Photo: Monica Spezia/Living Inside; p133l: Mark Anthony Fox; p133r: Photography: Tim Van de Velde/Photofoyer, Project: Karper by HE Architecture; p134l: Photos: Helenio Barbetta/Living Inside; p134r: Tessa Jol/Taverne Agency; p136: Lisa Cohen/Taverne Agency; p139: Photo: Monica Spezia/Living Inside, Styling: Fulvia Carmagnini, Owner: Sophie Wannenes – founder of Narkisso; p140–1: @ FLC/ ADAGP, Paris and DACS, London 2022. / @ ADAGP, Paris and DACS, London 2022, Photo: Nathalie Krag/Living Inside, Styling: Roberta Brambilla, Interior Designer: Studio 2046; p142–143: Jansje Klazinga/Taverne Agency; p144l: Tessa Jol/Taverne Agency; p144r: Photography: Fabrizio Cicconi/Photofoyer, Styling: Francesca Davoli, p145–153: Mandy Lee; p155: Taran Wilkhu; p157–159l: Mark Anthony Fox; p159r: Photo: Monica Spezia/Living Inside, Styling: Fulvia Carmagnini, Owner: Sophie Wannenes – founder of Narkisso; p160: Michael Sinclair/Taverne Agency; p161: Charles Urmston; p162: Photo: Monica Spezia/Living Inside, Styling: Fulvia Carmagnini, Owner: Sophie Wannenes – founder of Narkisso; p163: Michael Sinclair/Taverne Agency, Styling: Laura Fulmine; p164–165: Charles Urmston; p167: Photo: Monica Spezia/Living Inside; p169: @ living4media/Are Media; p171: Photography: Fabrizio Cicconi/Photofoyer, Styling: Francesca Davoli; p172l: Mark Anthony Fox; p172r: Photo: Monica Spezia/Living Inside, Styling: Francesca Sironi, Owners: Founders of Nanban; p173: Photo: Christina Kayser O./Living Inside, Styling: Rikke Graff Juel; p175: Photo: Monica Spezia/Living Inside; p177l: Charles Urmston; p177r: Photo: Michael Paul/Living Inside, Owner: Joris Van Apers; p178–9: Anna Malmberg/Taverne Agency, Stylist: Mari Strenghielm; p180: Photo: Monica Spezia/Living Inside; p183l: Photo: Marco Bertolini/Living Inside, Owner: Kimberly Von Koontz, landscape designer; p183r: John Dummer/Taverne Agency; p185l: Anouk de Kleermaeker/Taverne Agency; p185r: Christine Bauer/Taverne Agency; p186: Photo: Johan Sellén/Living Inside, Stylist: Gill Renlund, Owners: Buster & Punch founders; p189–195: Graham Atkins-Hughes; p197: Charles Urmston; p199: Michael Sinclair/Taverne Agency, Styling: Laura Fulmine; p200: Anna Malmberg/Taverne Agency, Stylist: Mari Strenghielm; p201–202: Charles Urmston; p204: Michael Sinclair/Taverne Agency, Styling: Laura Fulmine; p207: Charles Urmston; p209: Michael Sinclair/Taverne Agency, Styling: Laura Fulmine; p210: Charles Urmston; p211: Anna Malmberg/Taverne Agency, Stylist: Mari Strenghielm; p212: Michael Sinclair/Taverne Agency, Styling: Laura Fulmine; p213: Anna Malmberg/Taverne Agency, Stylist: Mari Strenghielm; p215: Lisa Cohen/Taverne Agency; p217–218: Charles Urmston; p219: John Carey/Rosendale Design; p221: Photography: Nicole Franzen; p222: Anna Malmberg/Taverne Agency, Stylist: Mari Strenghielm; p225: Photos: Valetina Sommariva/Living Inside, Owner: Monica Damonte architect; p227: Lisa Cohen/Taverne Agency; p229–235: Photography: Fabrizio Cicconi/Photofoyer, Styling: Francesca Davoli.

# ACKNOWLEDGEMENTS

Writing my fifth interiors book was something I only ever dreamed of and I am so very grateful and thankful to everybody involved. Just like my business, it's not a solo journey; without so many incredible people this book simply would not have happened.

To Mummy and Daddy, thank you for being so incredibly supportive and for always being there, you are both such an inspiration. To the rest of my family, Gem, Hols, Russ, Lee, Lils, Thea and Jude, I love you guys so much. To G, who never gets fed up or down, who supports my every move no matter how crazy my ideas.

To my AA team: without you, none of this would be possible. You are the best and I really am the luckiest person to have you on board this ship; Cathie, Cordula, Gem, Hollie C, Hollie S, Imran, Jess, Maya, Megs, Nick, Russ and Shell.

To Rosie who makes my home the cleanest ever and has been part of our family for years we all love you, Monkey and Werts more than anything!

To my publishing team, Clare and Laura you have brought my vision to life thank you so very much. To Graham Atkins Hughes, my long-term bud, photographer and collaborator thank you for your lovely photographs.

To the incredible creatives whose beautiful houses we showcased:

Mandy Lee.

Gary Marshall (spatial and interior design) gymarshall@hotmail.com and Keith Hirst (structural steel work and staircase design keith.hirst@hfk.co.uk).

Jason Atherton (Rosendale Design, photography by John Carey).

Nate Berkus, interior designer and author, and Jeremiah Brent, interior designer, with photography by Nicole Franzen.

To Charlie Urmston who is such an integral part of team AA and takes the most beautiful pictures and the biggest shout out to Gem my sis, biz partner, best bud and voice of sanity. Lastly but so importantly everyone else, every single customer, follower, client and reader. Without your support this just wouldn't be possible and it means the world. Thank you xxx

Pavilion
An imprint of HarperCollins*Publishers*
1 London Bridge Street
London SE1 9GF

www.harpercollins.co.uk

HarperCollins*Publishers*
Macken House, 39/40 Mayor Street Upper
Dublin 1, D01 C9W8
Ireland

10 9 8 7 6 5 4 3

First published in Great Britain by
Pavilion, an imprint of HarperCollins*Publishers* Ltd
2022

ISBN 978-1-911682-36-3

Commissioning Editor: Lucy Smith
Managing Editor: Clare Double
Picture Research: Abigail Ahern and Sophie Hartley
Design Manager: Laura Russell
Layout Designer: James Boast

This book contains FSC™ certified paper and
other controlled sources to ensure responsible
forest management.

For more information visit:
www.harpercollins.co.uk/green

Printed and bound by RR Donnelley in China